THE SPORTING LIFE

LIFE

ALSO BY BILL BARICH

FICTION

Carson Valley

Hard to Be Good: Stories

NONFICTION

Long Way Home

A Pint of Plain

A Fine Place to Daydream

Crazy for Rivers

Big Dreams: Into the Heart of California

Traveling Light

Laughing in the Hills

THE SPORTING LIFE

LIFE

HORSES, BOXERS, RIVERS, AND A RUSSIAN BALLCLUB

Bill Barich

Skyhorse Publishing

First Skyhorse Publishing Edition 2016

The contents of this book first appeared, in a slightly different form, in *The New Yorker* except for "The Quarter Pole" and "Only the Bull" (*Sports Illustrated*), "Hat Creek Days" (*California* magazine), "Never Say Never" (*Missouri Review*), and "My Wicker Creel" and "The Mayflies of Lough Arrow" (*California Fly Fisher*).

Skyhorse Publishing books may be purchased in bulk at special discounts for sales promotion, corporate gifts, fund-raising, or educational purposes. Special editions can also be created to specifications. For details, contact the Special Sales Department, Skyhorse Publishing, 307 West 36th Street, 11th Floor, New York, NY 10018 or info@skyhorsepublishing.com.

Skyhorse Publishing® is a registered trademark of Skyhorse Publishing, Inc.®, a Delaware corporation.

Visit our website at www.skyhorsepublishing.com.

10 9 8 7 6 5 4 3 2 1

Library of Congress Cataloging-in-Publication Data is available on file.

Cover design by Tom Lau

Cover photos: iStockphoto

Print ISBN: 978-1-5107-0696-5

Ebook ISBN: 978-1-5107-0697-2

Printed in the United States of America

Contents

Preface

M<small>Y</small> FASCINATION with the sporting life began when I was growing up in a desolate Long Island suburb, where children were expected to amuse themselves at the playground or on the sandlot fields. As a boy, I indulged in endless rounds of baseball, basketball, and football, with games of stickball, stoopball, punchball, and Wiffle ball tossed in for good measure. I fished a little, as well, and tried boxing a few times, but the brief joy I felt in the ring vanished abruptly when a much tougher kid knocked me to the canvas (bloody nose, loose tooth) in a Police Athletic League bout. My future lay elsewhere, I decided right then, and I never donned the gloves again.

Horses came into the picture later, when I was a sophomore in high school and itching for some minor-league trouble. Our town was close to Roosevelt Raceway, where

the not entirely wholesome sport of harness racing is featured, and because some neighbors on my block viewed the
track as a symbol of degeneracy, I was eager to slip through
the turnstiles at the earliest opportunity. But before I could
pull it off, I became a junior gambler with the help of my
friend Eddie Greco, who was older than me and already
had a job in the real world that put him in touch with the
action.

Eddie worked the restaurant counter at a bowling alley
near Roosevelt, where the menu was long on burgers and
doughnuts. Included among his customers were a few sulky
drivers, who popped into the lounge for drinks, ordered
some food, and tipped my pal with betting advice instead of
money. The horses they touted ran remarkably well. I
learned about the scam when I bumped into Eddie at a
Friday-night party. He mentioned that the guys had just
alerted him to Rhythm Lad, a hot pacer scheduled to run
on Saturday.

"I've got him across-the-board," he bragged.

"How much does it cost?" I asked, never having heard
the words *across-the-board* before.

"Six bucks."

I dipped into my wallet. On Sunday morning, I nearly
jumped out of my skin when a copy of *Newsday*, our local
paper, thumped against the front door. There in the black
type of the racing charts I saw Rhythm Lad on top, paying eighteen dollars for the six I'd invested. Naturally, I

was keen to collect my winnings, so I called Eddie at the bowling alley around noon. But he let me down by saying he'd already parlayed the money on a second hot horse about to run. *Parlay* was another new word I added to my vocabulary.

In about a month, I had seventy-five dollars hidden in a shoe box in my bedroom closet. My lucky streak might never have quit, not with Eddie Greco at the helm, except that I got cold feet. My mother, a devout churchgoer, believed gambling was a sin, and if she caught me with the stash, I knew I'd be in for a terrible punishment—hours of washing dishes or, worse, enforced Bible study. So I got rid of my bankroll by lavishing gifts on my girlfriend, squiring her around our best shopping mall with all the subtle cool of a mobster showing off his bimbo.

I did visit Roosevelt in person, finally, even though I wasn't old enough to place a legal bet. Nobody ever checked my ID when I bought a ticket, though—only when I tried to cash one. This created a strange scenario, whereby I had to wander through the crowd in search of an honest-looking adult who might assist me without demanding a cut of the profits. Sailors in uniform proved to be particularly sympathetic, just as they were whenever an underage teen needed an ally to score a six-pack at the corner deli.

Harness racing failed to move me, I must admit. The sight of grown men speeding by in their rickety sulkies was more comic than engaging. It wasn't until I took the train to Belmont Park and stood by the rail with my heart pumping that I got hooked on horses for real. I loved the sheer animal grace on display, the brightly colored silks and the beauty of the pageant. I noticed, too, how during the fleeting time of a race, I had no interest in anything beyond the moment. What I'd discovered was a sort of release.

In rereading the pieces here, I can see that I still look to the sporting life for escape and maybe even transcendence, if that isn't too grand an idea. It can happen on a trout stream when I fall into the meditative grace of casting, or during the raw intensity of a good boxing match, or at a baseball game if enough is riding on the line. It's the electricity I crave, a bolt from the blue that burns the fuzz from my brain and reminds me that I'm still alive and kicking.

I continue to follow the horses now and then, if only to see where they'll lead me. In every country, racing offers a vivid cross-section of the population and an instant introduction to the cultural norms. In Barbados, I once had to squeeze past a dreadlocked reggae band to place my wagers; in Florence, I enjoyed a wonderful meal of pasta and roast veal at a *tavola caldo* off the backstretch, where the patrons cared more about the food than the betting; in England I ate cockles and jabbered with Cockney bookies over the relative merits of steeplechasers; and in Louisiana, way down in the bayous, I watched in awe as some Cajun jockeys strolled into the paddock guzzling cans of beer.

Another great benefit of the sporting life is the amazing array of people you meet. Although I never shook hands with Mike Tyson, I did chew the fat with Donald Trump and attended his "celebrity" bash in Atlantic City, where, after Iron Mike disposed of Michael Spinks in ninety-one seconds, somebody picked my pocket. Pat Lawlor, an Irish pug from San Francisco, treated me as a member of his family, while Andrei Tzelikovsky of the Moscow Red Devils sold me a nesting doll and gave me a pack of Soviet baseball cards as a bonus.

In the end, I suppose this book is merely another aspect of my curiosity about the world and what we make of it. How we play is who we are, at least to some extent. If pressed, I might even argue for the importance of the pastimes we devise and the relief they sometimes deliver. The human being who invented the ball will never be as celebrated as the wheel's inventor, but we should still value the contribution. I hope these stories reflect the pleasure I took in writing them, and convey it to the reader.

1
Chasers

I HAD NO INTENTION of playing the horses on a recent
vacation trip to London. Instead, my pursuits were
going to be cultural. From a Cockney broker, I rented an
apartment on Belsize Avenue, in Hampstead, and spent my
first few days touring the museums nearby. I saw the four-
poster John Keats slept in, read the bad reviews of his second book, and marvelled at the elegance of his handwriting.
Around the corner, I visited the house where Sigmund
Freud lived for the last year of his life and learned from a
tour guide that he'd been fond of such writers as Twain, Poe,
and Anatole France.

When I wasn't at museums, I was browsing in second-
hand bookstores on Charing Cross Road, or going to galleries
and attending concerts at the South Bank Centre. One
Sunday afternoon, I heard a chamber group perform a spir-
ited version of Schubert's "Trout" Quintet, and afterward,

as I walked a path along the Thames, I found this poem inscribed on a paving stone:

> Enjoy thy streame, O harmless Fish!
> And when an Angler, for his dish,
> Through gluttony's vile sin,
> Attempts, a wretch, to pull thee out,
> God give thee strength,
> O Gentel Trout,
> To pull the raskall in!
> —*John Wolcot, 1801*

As you can see, I wasn't wasting my time. In fact, I doubt whether I would ever have made a wager if I hadn't got caught in a freak rain shower on Haverstock Hill. I looked around for a museum, a gallery, or a concert hall to take shelter in, but all I could find was a Mecca betting shop.

There are Mecca shops in most parts of London. They have distinctive green signs and opaque windows to protect their customers from prying eyes. Hampstead is an upscale area, so I was surprised that the shop was packed, with about thirty people studying the racing pages tacked to the walls. I recognized a butcher from down the block, two waiters from a Chinese restaurant, and an old man who'd once stopped me at the Budgen supermarket and warned me not to buy any Greek vinegar, because it contained poison.

I don't know what the man had against the Greeks, but I can tell you that he had no qualms about endorsing greyhound racing, which is big business in England. To put it boldly, he was an absolute fiend for the dogs. I listened as he lectured a friend on the importance of an upcoming event at Hove, where Ballyregan Bob, a champion hound, would try to set a new world record by winning his thirty-second consecutive race. An American, Joe Dump, was the current record holder, but Dump posed no problem, since he was retired to stud in Alabama.

Frankly, I was not a fan of Ballyregan Bob's. His picture kept appearing in the tabloids, and the efforts of the media to catch him "smiling" or "laughing" struck me as yet another perverse attempt on the part of the British to elevate animals to the status of human beings.

At Mecca, I found that the National Hunt season was well under way. Horses were out on the circuit, jumping over hurdles and steeplechase fences at Doncaster, Cheltenham, and Kempton Park, and I felt a keen longing to be with them. I'd gone to some of those courses during earlier visits to England and had grown very attached to jump racing. I thought of it as an unspoiled form of sport, pastoral in character and smacking of the nineteenth century. If I closed my eyes, I could still get a clear image of the countryside where jump-race meetings usually take place—rolling green hills, trees with their last leaves of yellow and gold, and orderly little backyard gardens.

In the morning, to catch up on the scene, I bought a copy of England's premier racing paper, but the most fascinating story about jumping appeared in the *Times*. It recounted the strange case of Alex Whiting, a trainer whose horses were unable to win at his home track, in Nottingham. After much deliberation, Whiting had decided to blame his great-uncle Cyril. It seems that Cyril had ordered his ashes to be scattered over the course—whether in despair or celebration nobody knew—so Whiting engaged the services of Father Frank Shanahan, a Roman Catholic priest, to carry out a blessing. Father Shanahan sprinkled holy water near the finishing post, but two of Whiting's entries still lost the next day.

I felt a pang of sympathy for Whiting, since I have also been guilty of blaming my bad luck on, say, creatures from outer space. Actually, when I stopped in at Mecca that afternoon, I believe it was a weird pull in the tide, on the coast by Bristol, that caused me to put a pound to win on Professor Plum, who was thirteen years old—ancient even by the lax standards of jumping—and in his last outing had finished seventh in a field of seven. This was a terribly sentimental bet, drawing its energy from a detective board game I used to play when I was a kid, and as I listened to a broadcast of the race over the shop's loudspeakers I was sure that the Professor's dallying at the rear of the field was less tactical than geriatric.

But my afternoon did not turn out to be a total waste. One of the clerks at the shop told me that there would be a meeting at Ascot on the weekend, so in the evening I phoned some friends and proposed a Saturday outing to the track. I should have known better. My friends in London are all members of the political left, and they expressed disgust at the mere mention of Ascot and accused me of being a toady of the Queen's. I pointed out that we would be going to the humble jump races, not to Royal Ascot, which occurs in June; but they ignored me, and I managed to recruit just one friend in the end, Dr. Andrew Moss, who claims to be only half English, and hence only half subject to the ordinary prejudices.

This claim of Andrew's is based on the fact that he has lived in California for more than twenty years, or almost all his adult life. He was born in Hampstead and grew up in a left-wing family, but he met and married an American while he was a graduate student at the London School of Economics and moved with her to San Francisco. Although they are separated now, Andrew has stayed on in the United States, partly to be close to his three sons, who make him alternately proud and crazy. In spite of his early training, he did not become an economist. Instead, he drove a cab, played electric guitar, engaged in radical politics, worked as a book editor, wrote a novel, and then, somewhat unaccountably, returned to graduate school and became an epidemiologist and a university professor.

At any rate, Dr. Moss was in England on a well-deserved sabbatical. When I arrived at his apartment on Ascot Saturday, I was glad to see that a break had already done him some good. His mood was jolly and expansive. He'd earned some money as a consultant, he said, and that had led him to buy a real adult topcoat—his first—and a bright-yellow VW Rabbit with only a couple of dents.

We took the Rabbit to Ascot. The town lies roughly southwest of London, a few miles from Windsor Castle. Its race course was carved from a corner of Windsor Great Park at the request of Queen Anne, in 1711. That August, horses raced over it for the first time, competing for a purse of a hundred guineas and Her Majesty's Plate, which was made of sterling silver. Meetings continued on a regular basis until the Queen died, three years later—the day after her gelding Star won an event at York worth forty pounds. The action was sporadic for a while after that, but when the Duke of Cumberland moved to Windsor, late in the century, he revived Ascot, and it became a gambler's paradise featuring dicing, gaming, wrestling, and boxing in addition to thoroughbreds.

I always like to get to a racetrack before the first race, but Dr. Moss was in no hurry. It didn't bother him that he couldn't find Ascot on his map. Broad in the shoulders and padded in the girth, he has a constitution made for lounging on couches, for idle strolls by the Thames and long conversations over coffee or brandy. As we crawled through traffic in Hammersmith, inching toward the motorway, he treated me to a series of autobiographical asides, showing me such Mossian landmarks as the former site of St. Paul's

School, where he'd gone as a scholarship boy and been pushed around by nasty little Nigels and Basils. I appreciated the intimacy, but I kept glancing at the clocks on church towers and chip-shop walls.

As it happened, I needn't have worried. We had no more chance of arriving on time than Professor Plum had of finishing in front. We went too far on the motorway and got lost in a quaint suburb that seemed to consist of thousands of roundabouts. It was past noon when we saw a sign for Ascot, but instead of putting the gas pedal to the floor Dr. Moss slowed down and looked in disgust at several large mansions on the border of a wood that belonged to the Crown. Wealthy stockbrokers and attorneys lived in them, he said—men in bowler hats, who were perpetuating the evils of the class system and contributing to England's demise. I thanked him for the information.

We found a parking lot not far from the Ascot grandstand. From there, we dashed along a lane that led past some brick duplexes, all with homey plaques hanging over their doors. What is it that compels the English to give names to their country houses, even the most modest ones? "Cottage by the Dell." "Hut of Utter Harmony." "Hovel in the Glade." Andrew wondered if grooms might own the duplexes—or maybe exercise riders, or lads who worked on the grounds; but I do not come from an intellectual tradition that requires me to speculate on the purpose of every object in the universe, so I failed to pause and consider.

The stands at Ascot are divided into three sections, and we paid our way into the middle enclosure between the lowly Silver Ring and the regal Members'. On entering, I heard some cheering and knew that the first race must already be in progress. That proved to be true, and we had to watch it on a closed-circuit TV. I was a bit upset, really, but almost immediately I forgot about it and became involved in the lovely sight of horses jumping over fences. The turf on the course was a beautiful emerald color; the air was fresh and smelled of beer and pork pies; and I had a sense that I'd been delivered to the brink of a wonderful promise.

Winter days are brief in England, and so are the cards at jump meetings. Dr. Moss and I were under pressure and had only five more races on which to earn our fortune. From a vender, we bought programs, and I spent a minute studying the cover illustration of a race over Ascot Heath, circa 1760. A huge crowd of people in fancy clothes were bunched up at the fringes of the course, shouting and pointing as a black horse sped toward the finish, about five lengths ahead of everybody else. A few daring fans had climbed onto the roofs of carriages for a better view. In one corner of the painting, a gent in a frock coat lay sprawled on his back—a victim of drink or enthusiasm—and a peasant with a bundle of hay under his arm was thumbing his nose.

I opened my program to the pages for the second race and saw that they gave some handicapping information, as well as the usual data about jockeys, trainers, weights, and so on. Under each horse's name, in red type, there was a capsule appraisal of its record, along with tips on its condition and the sort of turf—firm, soft, heavy, yielding—it preferred. Together, Dr. Moss and I studied the material and agreed that we liked Nohalmdun, a five-year-old gelding whose owners had an obvious flair for puns. The Ascot tout assured us that Nohalmdun was a "very smart hurdler." Peter Scudamore, the finest rider around, would be handling him. What else did we need to convince us? After placing our bets with Jim Fish, a bookie from Portsea, we went back to the grandstand to watch the race.

White railings mark the track boundaries at Ascot. Rooks and blackbirds were flying over the course, flapping their shiny wings against a backdrop of cumulus clouds. From the winter parade ring, which is just below the stands, the jockeys took their mounts through a gate and onto the turf for a gallop. Nohalmdun looked trim and fit, and I felt certain that he wouldn't be inhibited by the distance of about two miles—as short as a race over hurdles ever gets. His jumping would not be a significant factor, either, because hurdles aren't as high or as rigid as steeplechase fences. If he made a small mistake, brushing one with his legs or belly, he'd recover in time to stay in contention.

But Nohalmdun turned in a flawless performance, in fact. He sailed over every flight, and when Scudamore urged him on in the stretch he accelerated and blew past the weary favorite, Barnbrook Again, so Dr. Moss and I considered ourselves perfect geniuses. Yet in the very next race our consensus was shattered, and I am sorry to report that the horse the good doctor chose, Out of the Gloom, prevailed, in a much longer hurdles race of about three miles and a quarter. Why am I sorry? Because my friend was growing smug. A novice at the track, he had fallen into the trap of believing that handicapping was an easy way to get rich. Possibly no punter has ever been as brilliant as Andrew in his moment of triumph. He saved himself from censure only by buying us a couple of bottles of light ale as a treat.

Such was his smugness that he read aloud to me from his program while we were waiting for the result to be made official. He had found a page describing the Royal Ascot Meeting, and he wanted to share its procedural absurdities with me. For instance, to gain admission to the most exclusive enclosure, where the lords and ladies go, a new applicant has to write to the Ascot representative at St. James's Palace, in London, and supply the name of a sponsor who has held a Members' voucher for—program boldface—**at least eight years.** The dress code was stringent, too. If a fellow did get in, he had to wear a military uniform or morning dress and a top hat; a woman had to be attired in a formal day dress and a proper and fashionable hat.

"I guess that means no *crowns,*" Andrew said, chuckling away. If his trip home had rekindled his love for London—

which is to San Francisco as a novel is to a short story—it had also made him remember the injustices of the society in which he'd grown up.

As for me, I had nothing against the Royal Family. I'd even paid two pounds at the National Portrait Gallery to see an exhibit commemorating Queen Elizabeth's sixtieth birthday. The rooms were full of elderly men and women, who spoke in whispers and knew everything about the Queen, including her shoe size. The portraits were all severely flattering, but I did get a kick out of one 1957 photograph of Lord Snowdon's. He'd posed the Queen and her Consort on a footbridge, duplicating an old pastoral scene, and had them smile down at their children, Charles and Anne, as they read by a brook. According to a caption under the photo, Snowdon had bought some dead trout to complete the tableau, but his housekeeper, Mrs. Peabody, came across them in the fridge and had mistakenly fried them for his breakfast.

One of the nicest things about jump meetings is that you can get so close to the animals. We walked to the paddock before the fourth race and stood only yards away from an area where grooms were doing the saddling up. This was the day's feature—a steeplechase of about three miles that had a standard running time of six minutes. The horses had to go twice around a course that included a water jump, two ditches, and seven fences. A corporate sponsor had contributed about seventeen thousand dollars toward the purse, and that had helped to attract twelve entries, including some of the best chasers in the land.

I had an eye out for West Tip, a strapping gelding, who'd won the Grand National, at Aintree. This is jumping's most spectacular and historic race—little Elizabeth Taylor (a.k.a. Velvet Brown) once won it on her horse, The Pye, and raked in a handsome profit for M-G-M. But West Tip still had a big gut on him from a long summer of grazing, and I figured he would be slow to round into shape. He had an indifferent air about him, too, as if he wanted to be back at the barn with his nose buried in a feed bag, so I turned instead to Castle Warden, who was slender, genuine, and coming off a good win at Kempton Park. I couldn't bring myself to bet on Door Latch, even though he'd won this same chase before, beating West Tip by eight lengths. For all his speed and stamina, Door Latch had a problem— he was a faller. In the Grand National last spring, he'd fallen at the first fence; and in his two most recent races he had also, as the program put it, come to grief.

Naturally, Dr. Moss would not credit my selection. He had an idea of his own, fixed and immutable, and that idea was Bucko, a nine-year-old gelding from Ireland. I have to admit that Bucko looked splendid. His blackish coat glowed in the late-afternoon light. There was something dandyish about him, something to inspire romance, and as he pranced around and shook his head I could feel the fans verging toward a swoon. His braided mane formed a decorative ridge along the nape of his neck, and I am not exaggerating when I say that he had a habit of batting his lashes and flirting with the crowd. Yes, Bucko was our pretty boy, but he did have some substance. He'd won a recent chase at Haydock, his trainer was hot, and a number of experts picked him in their columns. The local Ascot tout registered a dissent; he said that Bucko needed to improve to win in this company.

But Bucko was surely unaware of it. He showed no signs of intimidation, no tics or twitches. He left the paddock so high up on his hoofs that he could have been tap dancing. And whom should he meet in the parade ring but the Queen Mother! Oblivious of the temperature, she was standing there in a simple dress, without a robe or an overcoat to keep her warm. She wore gloves and a picture hat, and on her face I saw exactly the same expression I'd seen in all the portraits at the Portrait Gallery. The Queen Mother owns a string of jumpers herself, but none were in the race, and it occurred to me that her presence in the ring could scarcely be interpreted as a good omen for Dr. Moss, with his distaste for royalty.

While the Queen Mother chatted with officials, I went off to place my wager. Down by the rail, the Cockney bookies were raising their usual ruckus. They chalked their odds on slates, and the odds kept changing to reflect shifts in the action. Castle Warden was hardening, or dropping down, from eight to one, and I got him at seven to one from a bookie in a dark-blue embalmer's suit. (Bucko was the favorite, at seven to two.) Every bookie prefers dour colors, hoping to induce a depression in his customers. Anyway, this bookie accepted my five-pound note, dictated the terms of the bet to his scribe—an urchin who had the crabbed posture of Melville's Bartleby—and threw the cash into a leather satchel at his feet.

Ascot is a triangular, right-handed course, which means that horses travel it in a clockwise direction. The start of a three-mile chase is beyond and to the left of the stands. There is no gate, so riders mill around, circling and shopping for position, until the starter lowers the flag. Bucko didn't miss a beat. Andrew and I watched him roll out from the pack and take up a spot near the leaders, while Castle Warden lingered at the rear. They both jumped the first two fences easily, rising from the earth in an amazingly graceful way that struck me as incompatible with the species. Horses are not supposed to soar, but they do.

I'd neglected to bring my binoculars to England, and I soon regretted it. As the field crossed over the water jump and galloped into open country, I lost track of individual horses. I could make out shapes, but they were so reduced in size that the differences among them were obscured. To follow the horses' progress, I became dependent on the Ascot announcer, who, as you might expect, delivered his call in an unemotional British style. The lessons of the ages were in his voice; he could have been dispatching taxicabs.

Gradually, the horses came back into view, passing the stands and readying themselves for another circuit of the course. Bucko was in the midst of the hunt, striding along in limber fashion. He looked so elegant you would have thought he'd been engineered for this specific occasion. Door Latch was with him and so were Plundering and Broadheath, but Castle Warden was still at the rear of the pack and in need of a blowtorch held to his tail. I must have been squirming, because Dr. Moss glanced at me from what amounted to a superior plane of being; and he might have remained there forever, I think, if something untoward hadn't happened.

This had to do with Bucko. Quite suddenly, as the field ran into the country again, he began to droop and tire. He resembled a person who's just received a dose of bad news. His body slumped forward, and the other horses dashed by him. He was too far away from the stands for us to witness his accident, but we got word of it from the announcer. "We have a faller, ladies and gentlemen," he said, without a hint of pity. "It's Number Eight, Bucko." Apparently, Bucko had hit a fence with his legs and tumbled to the ground. I couldn't see the Queen Mother from where we were sitting, but I felt certain that she'd still have exactly the same expression on her face.

Dr. Moss did not make a scene about the tragedy. There were no tears or shrieks. He just crumpled his betting ticket and let it drop from his hand. Pretending to be a disinterested observer, above such concerns as winning or losing, he watched the horses enter the stretch, where they had two fences left to jump. Door Latch was in front now, but he was puffing, and when he got over the first fence—barely, landing on wobbly legs—the crowd applauded him. The next fence was a furlong away, and as he came to it he seemed to shut his eyes and surrender himself to fate. I thought of paratroopers, of children leaping from burning buildings. Then Door Latch was in the air, suspended above a thatch of gorse and birch; and he stayed there for a long time, floating, before he touched down and ran on.

There must be a dozen good reasons not to bet on a race known as the Frogmore Chase, but Dr. Moss and I paid them no mind, and after another trouncing we were faced with our last chance, in the form of the Hampton Court Hurdle. The conditions of the race were less than favorable. Twenty-three horses were entered, and some of them were fatter than West Tip. To make matters worse, the Hampton Court was restricted to amateur riders, with such names as Mr. J. Geake and Miss M. Mergatroid. I played Cats Eyes, because he had some class, but he got winded after a mile or so, and his rider, Mr. R. Bellamy, probably had to promise him a bunch of carrots just to get him to finish third.

Dr. Moss had a small bet on Red Rocky, who also ran in the money, and he earned enough to make his afternoon a financial success. We took our drive home at a leisurely pace. On the motorway, we passed a pond half hidden in reeds, and a flock of geese burst from it into the sky. Then we were in London again, watching the lights go on in the fine houses on Primrose Hill, and Andrew's nostalgia returned. The apartment he had rented was in a building he'd lived in as a child, and he couldn't unlock the door without recalling all the sights, smells, and textures of his family. The place must have looked awfully bare to him now; and though he told me he was anxious about the imminent arrival of his boys, who were flying over for a visit, I had a strong feeling he would survive.

At his supermarket, Dr. Moss can buy a whiskey, the Famous Grouse, that is as sound as knobby Brussels sprouts and King Edward potatoes. He brought out a bottle and poured two glasses. We sat at his only table, which was covered with letters, journals, and phone messages—items to be dealt with on another day. Andrew's middle son, Jesse, had left behind a Pink Floyd tape on his last visit, and Andrew played it on a tiny Sony tape machine that had speakers no bigger than matchboxes. I began to get a little nostalgic myself, saddened to be coming to the end of my vacation. I had an unnatural desire to go to Hove or Wembley for an evening of greyhound racing, but I repressed it. When my friend offered another splash of whiskey, I accepted, and we sat around and talked about Ascot and the horses until quite late.

2
Pride of the Sunset

HISTORY MATTERS enormously to most boxers. Ask any ring veteran about his career, and the first thing he'll mention are all the immortals he has traded punches with, even when he was on the losing end of the exchange. Sometimes it's enough for a fighter to be a footnote to great events, since that earns him a marginal place in the record books and rewards him with a repertoire of inside stories. In a sense, the stories are his capital, and if he's lucky he may parlay them into a business opportunity and open a tavern someday, after he retires—or so it goes in Irish Pat Lawlor's fantasy.

Lawlor is a San Francisco junior middleweight whose talents are not unlimited. Against the odds, he ekes out a living as a boxer in a city where boxing is less popular than origami. In many respects, Lawlor is a throwback to a bygone era, who would fit nicely as a bit player in a Jimmy

Cagney film. At the age of twenty-six, he has a boyish charm, although he acts like a tough guy around strangers. Handsome in the rugged way of cops and firemen, he has a square jaw, a lightly freckled face, and reddish-brown hair. When he puts on a favorite tweed cap—it looks as if a truck tire had crushed it—you figure he must be heading home to Donegal. His mind is strewn with boxing trivia, and he can recite the exact dates of all his bouts and will list, without much prodding, his three biggest thrills as a fighter: being carried from the ring after his first pro victory; getting a fan letter from West Germany; and fighting an exhibition match with Roberto Durán, a Panamanian immortal.

The exhibition took place at the Civic Auditorium in San Francisco. It's no understatement to say that Lawlor worshipped his opponent. In Durán he saw the epitome of what a boxer should be—a blend of savagery and soul. Four times a world champ, Durán started fighting in Colón when he was fifteen, and soon became known for his killer instinct. He seemed to view weakness in others as a personal affront, something intolerable in human beings which he'd been authorized to stamp out. In his prime, he had a body that appeared to have been carved from a granite mountain and set upon the earth in a single, indestructible piece. When Durán wasn't boxing, he lived like a playboy, hanging around night clubs until dawn or tooling about the dusty streets of Panama City in one of his five Alfa

Romeos. He loved eating steaks, drinking Johnnie Walker
Scotch, and dancing to salsa music, but in time this under-
mined his desire to train, and he would retire for a while,
then return for a fight or two, and then retire again.

It was Durán's most recent comeback attempt that had
led him to Pat Lawlor and the Civic. Financial concerns
motivated him. He owed the Internal Revenue Service
more than a million dollars, but he also hoped to erase a
blemish from his otherwise noble record. A ghost from the
past haunted him—Sugar Ray Leonard. He had suffered an
embarrassing defeat against Leonard while defending his
world welterweight title. Sugar Ray had bamboozled him,
taunting him with silly gestures and so upsetting him that
he quit in the eighth round, breaking a boxing taboo. *"No
más!"* Durán cried. The phrase followed him home to
Panama, where his surrender was interpreted as a national
disgrace, as well as an insult to machismo. Durán blamed it
on his stomach cramps. Before the bout, he had reportedly
stuffed himself with two eggs, grits, peaches, toast, an orange, two T-bones, peas, French fries, and a portion of fried
chicken, washing it all down with consommé, hot tea,
water, Kool-Aid, and four large glasses of orange juice.

Lawlor had heard about Durán's appetite, so he wasn't
surprised when the Panamanian arrived in San Francisco
weighing almost two hundred pounds, more than forty
pounds over his ideal weight. It puzzled him, though, because Durán had been trim and muscular in his last bout

when he won a split decision over Iran Barkley, a top middleweight, and reestablished his credentials as a contender.
The real question was whether or not this meant that Sugar
Ray Leonard would give Durán another title shot. Lawlor
hoped so, because he had no fondness for Sugar Ray. In his
opinion, Leonard was arrogant, a corporate type who played
ball with the TV networks and cut deals that were the envy
of every other boxer. Lawlor admired Leonard's skills, but
he did not approve of the man or his methods: Leonard was
too slick, too stuck up for his own good.

A crowd of about five thousand fans jammed the Civic—
a huge crowd by San Francisco standards. When Lawlor
climbed into the ring, accompanied by his aging trainer, Al
Citrino, he could have been stealing a scene from his favorite boxing movie, *Somebody Up There Likes Me*. He realized
that he might never again have such a moment, yet he didn't
feel that the moment was undeserved. After all, he had a
perfect record of twelve wins and no losses. It was true that
he'd never faced a boxer of tested caliber—the fellows he
had beaten were often pulled in off the streets—but everyone had to start somewhere. Lawlor understood, too, that
most people in the auditorium had come to see Durán, but
a vocal contingent of his own supporters was also present,
distinguishing themselves by their hoots, their cheers, and
their shamrock-colored clothing.

One promise Lawlor had made to himself was that he
wouldn't challenge Durán or try to show him up. This

exhibition wasn't a real bout anyway, not with four two-minute rounds and pillowy, sixteen-ounce gloves. The point was to keep Durán busy and in the public eye until Leonard could be pinned to a contract, so when Durán seemed content to kid around, Lawlor sparred listlessly and never pressed for an advantage. Better to make a friend than an enemy, he thought. He was ecstatic just to be in the ring with a true champion, amazed that such a flabby man, now thirty-eight years old, could be so graceful. Durán wore a T-shirt to hide his belly, but the extra pounds did not hamper his punching ability. At one point, he backed Lawlor into a corner and tattooed him with combinations, all put forth with terrific speed. Lawlor accepted the blows not as punishment but as taps from a realm beyond the ordinary, where, in the not too distant future, he hoped to dwell himself.

The exhibition forged a bond between Irish Pat Lawlor and Roberto Durán, linking them, however loosely, in the annals of the ring. In exchange for his gentlemanly behavior Lawlor had gained a story about drinking beer with Durán after the show, out at the Boathouse, a sports bar where young Irish-Catholic men pursue young Irish-Catholic women. Durán had even visited Newman's Gym, in the Tenderloin, where Lawlor trains, and he shook hands and signed autographs. The Panamanian was a class act, so when Lawlor learned that a deal for a Leonard-Durán rematch had indeed been made he was very happy for his new friend. The fight was to be held in Las Vegas and the boxers would split about twenty million dollars, with Leonard getting the lion's share.

By coincidence, Lawlor also had an upcoming fight, his thirteenth, scheduled for the Cow Palace. He was to meet Drafton Bunch, a journeyman from San Diego. For *his* effort, though, Lawlor would only be paid fifteen hundred dollars. The line on Bunch was that he had a weak chin, but this turned out not to be the case. Bunch could take a punch, and he could also toss one. For three rounds, he eluded Lawlor, trash-talking all the while. "What say, Pat?" he'd coo. "You want some action?" Then, out of the blue, he landed a powerful right in the sixth round that caught Lawlor on the temple and sent him to the canvas for the first time ever as a pro. He rose quickly to his feet and proceeded to rally, but Bunch played it cool and cute, evading contact and working just enough to stay ahead on the judges' scorecard.

Lawlor took the loss hard. He went home a changed fighter, undefeated no more. He knew that a record of twelve and one created a vastly different impression from a record of thirteen and zero. Sometimes he was able to see the vanished zero in a positive light, as the lifting of a burden. Other boxers might not pursue him so aggressively now, or be so eager to beat him. But then his mood would grow dark, and he'd get angry about losing (though in his heart he believed that he had won) and would curse himself for agreeing to fight Bunch at all. Al Citrino had warned him not to, and anyway he should have been more cautious, since it was his thirteenth bout—unlucky thirteen! His pals consoled him by saying that at least he had survived a knock-down, but Lawlor, splitting hairs, replied that surviving hadn't been his intention. He had wanted to win. Besides, he didn't think he had really been knocked down. His feet had slipped, he said, and he had fallen.

About the only thing that lifted Lawlor's spirits was the prospect of watching the Leonard-Durán rematch on television. That's what he told me when I visited him a couple of days before the big event, at the house he rents in the Outer Sunset, a fogbound neighborhood by the ocean. The Irish have always lived out there in large numbers, maybe because the melancholy weather reminds them of home. They send their kids to Holy Name School, and the kids grow up and often stay put instead of moving away. There are many dark, cubbyhole bars around, where patrons are offered penitential gloom and Guinness from the keg, and also shops that sell soda bread and imported oatmeal to recent immigrants still nostalgic for the Old Country.

I found Lawlor padding around his underfurnished living room, licking his wounds—he had a black eye and a sore wrist—and planning a fight-night party for his buddies. He wore sweatpants and a Jeff Beck Guitar Hero T-shirt, and his feet, size 12, were bare. It was a typically chilly Sunset day, and Lawlor was burning newspapers in his fireplace, feeding sheet after sheet to the flames until his hands were black with ink. He had hoped to spar at Newman's that afternoon, but his car, a used Mazda, wouldn't start, even though he'd banged on the engine with an empty beer bottle, so he had some free time to chat with me.

He sat in a battered recliner and began by telling me how much he enjoyed running on the beach. "I love doing roadwork, but I have trouble with it," he said, showing off a surgical scar on his right calf. "My hamstrings and tendons are real tight. It's like a birth defect. When I was a boy, I had three operations. One at five, one at nine, and one at fourteen." He paused to scratch his head. "You know what I need to work on most? My concentration. I never should have lost to Bunch." The dread Drafton seemed to materialize in the room, and Lawlor hit him with a phantom combination, boom-boom. "I was only fifty percent that night.

"Next year, I'm getting serious about my career," he went on. No more beer and no more pizza. Pizza I eat like three, four times a week. Always the same pizza. Pepperoni, mushrooms, and barbecued pork. They say it's bad for you, but people die from eating good food, too." He grinned and hit Bunch with another phantom shot. "You know what I need to develop? A killer instinct like Durán's. I've been too nice of a guy."

The phone rang. It was Lawlor's mother, who lives nearby, calling about the menu for the party. After fielding her questions, Irish Pat dashed to his bedroom and came back with his West German fan letter, handling it tenderly. A fellow named Gerd claimed to be "delighted and thrilled" with Lawlor's "fine young ring life" and asked for an autographed photo. Gerd signed himself "Sportingly yours."

I noticed that the letter had a magical effect on Lawlor, as if it confirmed a unique vision he had of himself. A high-school dropout, somebody for whom books are a form of torture, he had never dreamed he would receive such mail, especially from a foreign country. It was easy to picture the letter in a frame, displayed on the wall next to the oil painting of Irish Pat that already held an honored spot. Boxing had opened up a world to him, in fact, bringing enlightenment and experience, and though he had to train diligently and work at odd jobs—unloading trucks or moving furniture—to make ends meet, he couldn't imagine a better way to live.

"My mother's cooking lasagna," he told me, flopping into the recliner again. "Lasagna, garlic bread, stuff like that. It'll cost me over a hundred dollars, but it's going to be a great fight. I like Durán to win. Leonard's a runner, and runners tire before trackers. Around the ninth, or maybe the tenth, Durán will catch him and probably knock him out. You come around here and watch with us. You'll meet my friends—everything from choirboys to cutthroats. There'll be a lot of girls. Believe me, you'll have a wonderful time!"

On the appointed night, I was indeed back at Lawlor's house. He had set up his TV in the middle of the living room, and it was transmitting images of a vacant boxing ring outside the Mirage Hotel, in the Nevada desert, where the temperature had dropped into the forties. According to an announcer, Sugar Ray was a nine-to-five favorite, but there was still plenty of money bet on Durán. I liked Durán myself, thinking he resembled the old Brooklyn Dodgers—a little weird, a little ragged, quite possibly in need of divine intervention. If he were to lose, the argument went, he would let down his countrymen again and cause blood to be spilled in the streets of Panama. Incentive enough, then, to trade punches for real.

Lawlor's guests began showing up in the early evening. The first to arrive was his dentist. A neighborhood soccer coach came next, followed by a sturdy light heavy from Newman's. A steady stream of young men in their twenties, all former Holy Namers, kept rolling in, greeting each other with shouts and high fives. They were a rough-and-tumble crew, and when they went to a bout of Irish Pat's—Lawlor sold them the tickets himself, taking a cut of the profits—they often became crazed and moderately violent, forming themselves into a beer-soaked human juggernaut that moved through auditoriums thrashing anything in its path.

Lawlor was in his element, all right, surrounded by his admirers. Among his pals he strolled, looking princely, a bottle of Bud in one hand and his tweed cap on his head. He had spent the day cleaning his quarters, and now there were no empties cluttering counters and no moldy sweat-clothes anywhere. The kitchen smelled of garlic and oregano, and the bathroom almost sparkled. As he circulated, Irish Pat gave off a vibration of utter happiness. If a woman flirted with him, he flirted back. He knew himself to be more fit than anyone else in the room, more daring, better prepared for the long haul. For a boxer this physical prowess is the true bottom line, and it lent Lawlor an extra dimension. There is a subtle calculus in the absorbing of blows, and so far he was still on the right side of the ledger, relatively intact and undamaged. He was not a champ, surely, but among his Sunset home boys he had the look of one.

Unfortunately, the same could not be said of Roberto Durán. I was dismayed to see how scrawny the Panamanian looked on entering the ring in Nevada. Durán had shed the necessary pounds, but his arms were scrawny, and he seemed tentative about the adventure that lay ahead of him. It must have unnerved him to watch Sugar Ray Leonard parade down an aisle in a karate outfit and a black knit cap, as if intending to foil Durán with the martial arts before committing a criminal act upon him.

The bell sounded, and the boxers confronted each other gingerly, feeling each other out. Leonard danced and skipped, then darted in to land quick lefts and rights that did no particular harm. If he had lost a step or two because of age, it did not matter. He was still too fast for Durán, who stalked him predictably, trying to get close and force Sugar Ray to brawl. Durán was flat of foot, a plodder beating to death a single idea, somebody in whom a saving bit of intelligence was not about to bloom.

His performance didn't sit well with the fans at Lawlor's house, either. Why didn't Durán use his big punch, a right that had crippled opponents in the past? "Throw the right," Lawlor urged him, demonstrating. Against the evidence, everyone continued to believe that Durán would wake up any minute, but as the rounds went by it became clear that he was over the hill. He couldn't connect with Leonard, could scarcely touch him. Instead, he kept getting hit, sometimes solidly enough to wobble his legs. The only bother to Leonard were small cuts above his eyes and inside his lip. Otherwise, he was in charge. He even clowned around a little, baiting Durán and coasting to an easy victory. It was a sorry spectacle—a real stinker of a fight—and when it ended there was nothing for Lawlor to do but turn up the volume on his stereo and rinse the bad taste from his mouth with another beer.

On Saturday morning, Al Citrino, who is seventy-nine, unlocked the door to Newman's Gym and waited for Pat Lawlor to come in for a training session. The gym is an unadorned place with a plank floor, mirrored walls, punching bags, and a ring whose canvas has been patched repeatedly with duct tape. A buzzer goes off at intervals—three minutes, one minute, three minutes, one minute—so that men who are shadowboxing can count the rounds. In a small office at the back, there's a photo of Citrino taken when he was trim and dapper, and all the hair on his head was brown. A survivor of 142 pro bouts, he once boxed the legendary Henry Armstrong and suffered a TKO. I asked him to describe Armstrong's style. "Busy," he said wryly. "Very busy."

Lawlor wandered in around nine-thirty, toting a gym bag that held his gear. His eye was less black, and he swore that his wrist felt fine. He stripped to his trunks and a T-shirt, put on his boxing shoes, and began to do some stretching.

"So what about the fight the other night?" Citrino asked him.

Lawlor snorted in disgust. "Seven million dollars," he said. "Durán should not *even* have been paid."

In boxing, there is an unwritten rule that forbids the belaboring of the obvious. A bad fight is allowed to recede into the mists, so everyone can sustain the illusion that the sport involves an unbroken string of superlative matches. Dempsey versus Tunney. Ali versus Frazier. Hagler versus Hearns.

When Lawlor had worked up a sweat, he donned some training gloves and started hitting a bag. Citrino observed and suggested pointers, at the same time conversing with Chuck Burkhardt, who works in Lawlor's corner when he fights. Chuck is seventy-one years old. There are no middle-aged people at Newman's, just old men, young boxers, and ghosts. The old men remember when you could attend a match in the Bay Area almost every night of the week. Bouts in Oakland, in San Francisco, in San Jose, and in

Sacramento. Bouts at a joint called Dreamland, which later became a skating rink called Winterland, which later became a rock-and-roll venue, and is now a condominium complex.

"In 1938, when I fought Armstrong at the Civic, we drew about fourteen thousand," Citrino said to Chuck.

"That's a nice crowd."

"Sure it is. You take Pat here, Chuckie, he's a fair fighter, he could become a draw. But the promoters don't help him. They should put him in against a guy with a big name who's on the way down. Know what I mean?"

"Sure," Chuck said. "Guy on the way down."

Citrino towelled the sweat from Lawlor's brow, and Lawlor stepped into the ring to shadowbox. Sometimes he imagined he was fighting Marvin Hagler. Sometimes Rocky Graziano.

"How you feeling, Pat?" Citrino asked.

"I feel real good, Al."

"Well, you look good. You didn't get tired when you went eight rounds against Bunch, did you?"

"Hell, no. I'd go twenty rounds against that son of a bitch."

"You think you can go ten, Pat?"

"Any time."

"You go ten rounds, you're going to have to be a good boy, you know. No beer, no pizza. You going to be a good boy?"

Lawlor smiled. "Sure," he said. "In the new year."

* * *

For boxing fans, the new year started with an amusing fiasco in Atlantic City that featured two aging heavyweights, George Foreman and Gerry Cooney, pretending that they were legitimate contenders for a title shot instead of entertainers out to fool the public. Cooney claimed to have triumphed in his battle against drugs and alcohol, but he boxed so clumsily that a little substance abuse might have helped him to cut loose. Foreman, whose forty-second birthday loomed on the horizon, floored him in short order. A preliminary bout between Doug DeWitt and Matthew Hilton provided far more action, even though Hilton, like Cooney, was recuperating from too many days spent in too many bars.

It was only natural for Lawlor to hold a party for the Foreman-Cooney fight. Once again his friends and his family gathered to have dinner and comment on the fine points, such as DeWitt's nose, from which, rumor had it, all the bones had been surgically removed to ease the boxer's breathing. Again, Lawlor circulated around the living room, but he sipped a soft drink and looked purposeful now, preparing himself for a rematch with Drafton Bunch at the end of January. He also announced that he had a new pen pal—an elderly fighter from Rochester, who had conducted his career under the name of Irish Pat *Lawler*. This Lawler had sent a picture of himself sitting next to Jersey Joe Walcott at a banquet, and it was passed from guest to guest, along with an autographed glossy of a *Penthouse*

Pet, who admired Pat and wanted a date. That caused Lawlor to blush, while he accepted congratulations on his good fortune.

To get ready for the rematch, Lawlor hired Eric (the Prince) Martin as a sparring partner. Martin was black and experienced, and he had a jivey style that was similar to Bunch's. Lawlor studied a videotape of the first fight, too, watching it over and over, so that he could learn from his mistakes. He concentrated as hard as he was able, even dreaming about Bunch and his demise, and when Bunch flew up from San Diego and bragged on a radio program that he planned to bust his opponent's jaw, it only served to fuel Lawlor's dedication. He felt that he had something important to prove, but then, at the last minute, Bunch pulled out of the bout, claiming that his ribs were bruised.

It was futile to guess whether or not Bunch was telling the truth, of course. Boxers often concoct ailments, suddenly becoming as delicate as Victorian maidens, in the hope of prying some extra cash from a promoter—in this case, two promoters, Jimi Sosa and Jimmy Keith. Though Sosa and Keith have been around the block, they are still subject to fits if somebody attempts to rob them, so they began a frantic search to replace Bunch, calling around the American West and cutting a deal first with Ali Sanchez, which fell through, and then with Eric McNair, which fell through, and then, finally, with Virgil Green, a fighter from Richmond, across the Bay Bridge. So Lawlor, disappointed and left in the lurch, had just four days to devise a new plan of attack, knowing absolutely nothing about Green except that he was a big hitter. "If you're still standing after three rounds, Pat," Jimi Sosa advised him, "you'll have a chance."

Such advice rests uncomfortably on a boxer's shoulders. When Lawlor got into the ring at the Civic, he did not appear overanxious for the fight to start. Green was a lanky, rough-looking customer, with long arms, ripply stomach muscles, and hair done in tight cornrows. He wasted no time in hammering Lawlor, bloodying his nose and working on his body, and leaving inflamed blotches on Irish Pat's skin. For a while, it seemed that Lawlor would go down. He did slip in the second, doing an awkward flop to the canvas, but he managed to make it through the round and then the next, and, slowly gathering confidence, he pounded Green's body in return, catching him in the head with a solid right that must have set the birds to twittering. His approach lacked grace and finesse, demonstrating instead the virtues of honest toil. Soon Green began to tire, to look less menacing and more bedraggled, and Lawlor kept after him, pushing him against the ropes and exerting enough control to win a unanimous decision.

As a sport, boxing is so full of paradox and so riddled with ironies that it tends to bring out a philosophical streak in fighters, and Irish Pat Lawlor's mood was indeed philosophical in the wake of his victory. Money problems were foremost in his mind. In taking on Green, he had signed for an eight-rounder—not the ten-round feature he would have had with Bunch—and the promoters had docked him nine hundred dollars. He'd also accepted some tickets on account from Keith and Sosa, but he had failed to sell very many and that left him twelve hundred dollars in the hole. When the sum was deducted from his already whittled-down purse, he would earn exactly four hundred dollars for beating poor Virgil.

"I'm never going to sell tickets again," he told me, on my last visit to his house. "No way! You know what happened? My friends, they all showed up at the Civic, but they bought tickets at the gate instead of from me. I lost my ass. I invite those guys over to a party, I feed them, and they say, 'Yeah, sure, Pat, I'll buy a ticket next week.' It's frustrating. I need a haircut, but I don't know if I can afford one." He let out a weary sigh. "Well, I may be broke, but I'm still happy I won. I could have performed better, though. It was a show of heart, not of skill. The public enjoyed it. Green tried, at least. I went up to him afterward and said he could have a rematch any time. You know what *he* said? 'Hey, man, I don't want any rematch with you.'

"In a couple of months, I might fight for a new promoter," Lawlor continued. "A guy up in Petaluma. I have to keep working. Get in there, get myself ranked by one of the organizations, then maybe fight for a title. Did you ever hear of the World Boxing Association Intercontinental junior-middleweight title?"

"No," I said.

"Anyhow, Ron Amundsen, he has the title now. I saw the championship belt on TV. It's beautiful, man, all blue and gold." Lawlor's thoughts turned toward history, toward the familiar longing of human beings to make something special of themselves. "That's really all I want from life. A chance to fight for a title. I don't want to go on doing this forever, you know?"

3
Hot Creek
Days

IT'S NO SECRET THAT Hot Creek is among the finest and most challenging dry-fly streams in the West. I had a chance to fish it for the first time not long ago, just after the season opened, in company with my friend Paul Deeds, who farms prunes on a forty-acre spread in Sonoma County. Deeds is a high-strung type, so he worried that we might run into bad weather and die in one of those freak blizzards that sometimes blow through the Sierra Nevada in early spring, but I chastised him for being overly sensitive and something of an old maid. That convinced him he ought to make the trip, of course, even if it went against his better judgment.

We met in San Francisco and followed a route through Yosemite National Park, where the weather indeed turned sour. An icy wind was howling, and snow began falling while we were crossing Tioga Pass. As the flakes hit our windshield, Deeds laughed bitterly, his gift of prophecy confirmed. "I hope you brought your mittens," he said, repeating himself a few times for effect. Here was rural humor at its best. You can always count on Deeds to rub it in. There isn't a slight he's ever suffered that he hasn't repaid over and over again.

The snow quit when we dropped down from the stratosphere and left the park, turning onto Highway 395. We went by June Lake and over Deadman Creek. "You'd think they would have more imagination," Deeds grumbled. "Deadman Creek! Somebody's been reading too many Westerns." When he saw a sign for Hot Creek Ranch, just beyond the town of Mammoth Lakes, we left the highway for a private road and soon came to a sweeping meadow. Hot Creek cut through it, snaking about in wide curves and oxbows. It wasn't a very broad stream, no more than twenty-five feet across at any point. Nine A-frame cabins were arranged along it, looking out on black mountain peaks dusted with fresh powder.

The ranch manager had a big house on the meadow. We found him out on his lawn, tinkering with a motorcycle he uses to patrol the property for trespassers. He wiped the oil from his fingers, had us register, and assigned us a cabin. It had a nice front porch with a view of the mountains and came with a library of old magazines and paperback books. Even before we had carried in our groceries, Deeds took over the kitchen table to sort through his tackle. I've never met anybody more eager to be on the stream. He was blind to world affairs, politics, natural disasters, and even movie-star gossip. All he cared about was catching fish.

We walked to the creek in the early evening, after the wind had died down. It was still very cold, with a prospect of frost on the menu. We wore sneakers instead of hip boots because wading isn't allowed on the ranch. The idea is to protect the delicate weed beds that provide cover for brown and rainbow trout, as well as supply them with oxygen. The trout in Hot Creek are famous for being wary and selective. They don't so much strike a fly as stop it for a moment, and if you don't set the hook right away, you've missed your opportunity. All of the creek is catch-and-release, so most trout have been hooked a few times, and that makes them even more finicky. You would be, too, after a trip or two into the open air.

We crossed an old wooden footbridge and paused by a quiet pool at the base of a chalky bluff. Deeds tied an elk-hair caddis to his twelve-foot leader and made a cast upstream, in the classic dry-fly tradition. The caddis landed lightly on the surface, as a newly hatched insect might, and drifted back toward Paul in a smooth, straight path, bobbing on its bristly wings. As the tiny fly approached, Deeds gathered up slack line in his free hand and cast again, letting the leader unfurl in an elegant loop. It had the quality of skywriting, leaving behind a wisp of itself, an image on the retina that slowly disappeared.

I moved to a spot where the creek was more narrow, some twenty yards away. For a few minutes, I stood very still and watched for bugs, but none were hatching—it was far too cold. Under such conditions, trout stay deep and have to be teased into hitting wet flies or nymphs fished below the surface, but Hot Creek Ranch only permits the use of dries. (These rules can be a pain, but they protect the resource and guarantee its survival.) I tied on a caddis imitation of my own and started casting blind, but I lacked faith and could have been tossing a stone into a well, hoping to hit an unseen target on the bottom. I could feel the snow on the mountains, too, an arctic blast that numbed my fingers and toes.

While I was daydreaming about margaritas and bonefish in the Florida Keys, I heard a noise behind me and saw an extremely ancient angler puffing back to his cabin. He must have been in his eighties. As he trudged along, he cursed the meadow, the creek, the elements—pretty much anything he could think of. He was a former banker from Santa Barbara and told me he'd gotten attacked by a hailstorm that morning, pelted with celestial golfballs. This was the worst weather he'd witnessed in thirty years of visiting the ranch, he said. He couldn't wait to crawl into bed, so he could pray for better conditions tomorrow.

"Only took ten fish all day," he complained, before going on. Ten fish sounded like a lot to me, and I wondered how he'd pulled off such a miracle.

Deeds is a country person and invariably wakes at dawn. Give him a kitchen to root through, and he'll bang on the pots, slice potatoes, crack open eggs, and whistle a medley of Bo Diddley tunes while he's fixing breakfast. By the time

I got up, he had a huge omelette cooking, along with a frying pan full of home-cured bacon. The cabin smelled as good as a cabin can smell, I believe.

After we ate, Deeds patted his belly and smoked a dimestore panatela.

"How harmful can cholesterol really be?" he asked contentedly.

"Fairly harmful, if you trust the scientific research."

"I don't trust anything scientific," Deeds said. Yes, we were back in the caveman era, where truth was an aspect of desire.

As it turned out, the old banker's prayers had been answered. It was much warmer outside, without a cloud in the sky. The sun lit up the meadow, and bugs were hatching everywhere, both caddis and mayflies. I could see the trout from a long way off—big trout that were feeding actively, dimpling the water with their lips. Before our eyes, a trophy rainbow leaped from the creek to snatch an insect from the air—a feat of aerobic derring-do that had us fumbling for our gear. In just three casts, Deeds caught a fourteen-inch fish and held it up for me to admire before he released it. I tried a tiny gray sedge, size twenty, and a trout hit it with a vicious slash, only to spit out the hook and vanish.

A half hour later, I was still in the same place, stupidly casting the same fly to the same trout, in violation of a basic angling law. If you disturb the water, you're supposed to move on because you've spooked the fish. Yet even Deeds, who is an expert and probes every part of a stream in meticulous detail, wasn't having any luck. His first trout was his only trout, so he was plenty frustrated and said that he wished he had it in him to break the ranch rules and use a nymph. When I joined him farther along the creek, he was sitting on the bank with his hat off and studying a riffle.

"One cast with a hare's ear," he told me. "That's all I ask."

"They'll arrest you, Paul. You could do hard time."

"This *is* hard time." He pointed to a spot in front of us, where a fat-bellied brown hung in the current. "Makes you want a shotgun, doesn't it?"

Around noon, hungry and tired from our efforts, we started back to the cabin. Three other anglers fell into step with us, equally ready for lunch, and I saw that they, like my banker pal, were gents of a certain age—not quite eighty, maybe, but well into their seventies. "I feel like a goddamn kid with this bunch," whispered Deeds, who's pushing fifty. Obviously, the physical ease of fishing Hot Creek appealed to them. There were no boulders to climb over, and no fast water to rip your legs out from under you and send you to a watery death.

We traded pleasantries as we walked, and I was stunned to hear how well they'd done. They couldn't be more complimentary about the creek and what it had delivered. Trout upon trout, if they were reliable.

"They must have a secret," I said to Deeds, as he built himself a monumental hero sandwich.

"Sure, they do. It's called lying."

* * *

When the wind came up again that afternoon, nearly carrying away Deeds' rod in a gust, he stomped his feet and insisted that there had to be a more sheltered stream somewhere in Inyo County. Were we confined to Hot Creek, after all? Definitely not. We were bold adventurers and should be out exploring.

On a Forest Service map, he located the Owens River and judged it to be about seven miles away, so off we went into the crystal-clear alpine light. The road we took was dirt, or some weird amalgam of dirt, flint, old tin cans, and rusty sawblades, so the going was very slow. We had to proceed at a crawl to keep from shredding the tires. In ten minutes, we'd covered only a mile and were lost in a landscape dominated by the stinking odor of rotten eggs—the sulphury fumes of a hot spring.

There are hot springs all through the Sierra Nevada, particularly in areas of geological unrest. Some are no larger or deeper than a bucket, while others are as spacious as a suburban swimming pool. They occur in rocky outcrops, in lava beds and pine forests, and in small-town backyards next to chiropractic offices. This one was in a little park and offered us an oasis in the midst of dust, lizards, and sun-baked earth. Our map marked its source as Hot Creek Geyser. A dozen people were soaking in the spring, floating on their backs with their eyes closed.

Everyone thinks Californians are quick to strip naked in public, but that isn't always the case. The floaters were modest and wore bathing suits, in fact, so we went back to the cabin and put on ours. We had to climb down a long staircase to reach the hot spring, but oh! The water was soothing after our day of disappointment! It massaged every weary tissue in our bodies, and we melted into it, reduced to a blissful, quasi-piscine state.

"We'll get 'em tomorrow," Deeds said.

"Amen," I replied, praying like the banker.

The next morning, Deeds was already out on the stream when I woke up. Against the toaster, he'd propped a note. "Ate bacon, left eggs. Hope you didn't want bacon." I ate the eggs, drank some strong black coffee, and slipped into my fishing vest. The meadow grass was still dewy, and the creek was the color of slate beneath a ribbon of blue sky. As I crossed the footbridge, a pair of cinnamon teal swam out from under it, turning their heads this way and that to gawk at the passing world.

By eight o'clock, the temperature was in the low seventies. For once, insects of every kind were on the wing, skittering along the surface of the stream. They created a spectacle of mindless energy, born into the bright light and oblivious of the predators that lay waiting for them. Rainbows rose greedily to suck them in, as visible as the ducks. When trout are on the feed, they make a loud slurping noise, as if they were spooning up a bowl of soup, and an angler who is trying but failing to seduce them becomes nervous and upset—casting badly, swearing, and casting badly again.

One of my bad casts so disgusted me that I threw down my rod and kicked at the bank. My line kept drifting, though, swinging out below me in an arc, and my fly became soggy and heavy and sank into the weeds. Now it was a dry fly performing in the manner of a nymph, underwater— no rule against that at Hot Creek Ranch! When the line began to twitch, I snatched my rod and set the hook, reeling in a nice brown. On my next cast, deliberately, I let the fly sink at the end of its drift and picked up another trout.

Eager to share the discovery, I went looking for Deeds. He was by the chalky bluff, grinning and smoking a cigar. That meant things were going well for him. He'd mastered the dry-as-wet-fly gambit on his own, after watching the Santa Barbara banker haul in three rainbows in rapid succession.

"You get that old," he said, "I guess you don't much care if you're cheating."

"Probably he doesn't see it that way."

"A banker," Deeds snorted. "Wouldn't you know it?"

I'd like to say that we didn't do any more cheating ourselves, but we did. All through the day we let our dries sink, and caught and released good fish. At dusk, Deeds tended to the porch barbecue and fired up the mesquite. He had a pair of beautifully marbled strip steaks he rubbed with garlic and coated with crushed black peppercorns, while I fiddled with the radio and searched for a station that broadcast something other than hog futures. On a clear night in the mountains, you can pull in programs from every Western state, and we wound up listening to a minor-league ballgame from Albuquerque, soothed by the familiar rhythms of the play-by-play.

Our long weekend came to an end the next afternoon. We loaded up the car and swept the cabin clean. On any stream, if the fishing goes well, there's a moment when you reach a plateau of satisfaction. You sit on a bank to rest, lean your back against a tree, and feel liberated from the many concerns of your daily life. For a brief time, you've earned a chance to simply exist, on a par with the birds, the grasses, and the trout, and it was this moment, more than any other, that we took home with us, along with the left-over groceries and the leaders still in their packages.

4
Going to
the Moon

WHENEVER THE Moscow Red Devils go barnstorming through a foreign country, they bring along twenty baseball players, a manager, a couple of coaches, and an equipment wrangler named Arkady, who has a bristly crewcut and often dresses in jeans and a leather flight jacket bearing an insignia patch from the fire department of West Babylon, New York. In some ways, Arkady is as important to the team as German Gulbitt, its crack pitcher, because he is in charge of selling the souvenirs that provide the Red Devils with some extra cash to supplement their monthly salary of roughly two hundred and fifty rubles.

Before each game, Arkady grabs a prominent spot in the grandstand and spreads out his wares, which include lacquered boxes, nesting dolls, cheap bracelets, Red Army hats, Rasputin caps of fake fur, Red Devils baseball cards, and a variety of Soviet watches that do everything from registering blood pressure to gauging barometric pressure. There is a set price for every item, of course, but it is set in Arkady's head and can be adjusted, depending on demand. On the March afternoon when I first met him, while the Red Devils were playing an exhibition game at Diablo Valley College, east of San Francisco, he was bargaining with a woman over the price of a nesting doll in the shape of Mikhail Gorbachev.

"Expensive in Russia," he said. "You can pay twenty-five dollars?"

"Well, I don't know," the woman replied, sounding as if she were worried about buying a Communist knickknack.

Arkady lifted Gorby and broke him apart to reveal a smaller doll inside. "Look, Brezhnev." Arkady smiled. Inside Brezhnev was Nikita Khrushchev. Inside Khrushchev was Joseph Stalin. And inside Stalin was a very tiny Vladimir Lenin.

"How about twenty dollars?"

"Sure," Arkady agreed, tossing in a hammer-and-sickle pin.

The Red Devils were making a whirlwind two-week tour of some junior colleges and high schools in the Bay Area, and Diablo Valley was their third stop. I had looked them up after reading a little piece about them in a San Francisco newspaper. It told how a customs inspector at the Moscow airport had interrogated Andrei Tzelikovsky, their right fielder, about the strange wooden object he was carrying—a baseball bat. Tzelikovsky explained that it was for playing an American sport. "I'm going to play baseball in United States," he added, to which the inspector, still eying the bat, inquired, "Tell me, how far are you supposed to throw it?" After that, Tzelikovsky and the other ballplayers passed successfully through security, survived an arduous flight, and were now boarded at a Marriott Hotel in San Ramon, an East Bay suburb, where their rooms, outfitted with cable TV, executive-style desks, and miniature bottles of shampoo, were more opulent than anything in Moscow.

For a while after arriving, the Red Devils had suffered from jet lag, which was complicated by the newness of everything they saw in San Ramon—clean, sparkling buildings everywhere, all of them untouched by the perils of time—and although they claimed to be over their symptoms, they were still having some trouble on the ballfield. They had dropped their first two exhibition games by wide margins, and the scoreboard at Diablo Valley showed that they were behind by twenty-one runs in the top of the seventh inning.

That was to be expected, perhaps, since the Red Devils, for all their enthusiasm, are probably not much better than a top-notch high-school team in the United States. But at the same time, it was a far cry from their performance at home the previous season, when they'd won all but two of their twenty-eight games and had defeated their arch-rivals, the Red Army club, to take the baseball championship of the U.S.S.R.

Baseball is such a new sport in the Soviet Union that discrepancies are bound to occur. The Russians love gymnastics, they wax poetic over soccer, but to date most of them have not been tempted to pick up a mitt or put on a pair of spikes. Until the era of *glasnost*, in fact, you could have driven from Ashkhabad to Zyryanka without ever bumping into anybody playing catch. Only when the International Olympic Committee voted to make baseball part of the Olympic Games did the Soviet authorities decide to sponsor teams. The Red Devils began their efforts the following spring with a modest advertisement in a Moscow sporting gazette, which invited interested athletes, gifted or merely courageous, to attend a training camp at a local university.

Andrei Tzelikovsky was among the first to report. He is the team's best speaker of English, so he was acting as its spokesman on the California tour. (Most Red Devils have acquired only one complete English sentence, which is "Would you like to buy this?") Tall, fair-haired, and broad-shouldered, with an innocent, boyish face, Tzelikovsky looks younger than he is—twenty-two—even though he carries himself with an astonishing seriousness of purpose. This was his fourth trip to the States, and he was starting to learn the media ropes. When we were introduced, I tested his grasp of the vernacular by commenting that he was "getting a lot of ink," and he just blinked, nodded resolutely, and said, "Ya, ya, I know." He has a profound sense of the game's traditions and its lore, which has led him to adopt, in homage, a bad habit: he chews tobacco (Red Man) mixed with shredded bubble gum, spitting so stylishly that his all-time favorite player, Shoeless Joe Jackson, would be proud.

Tzelikovsky has a knack for telling a story, and he once explained to me how he developed his unusual affection for baseball. He said that at the age of six he was admitted to a Red Army volleyball academy in Moscow, where talented children are groomed for stardom. But four years later his father accepted a post with the Soviet trade mission in Montreal, and the family moved. By chance, the Tzelikovskys rented an apartment right across from the Montreal Expos' stadium, and almost immediately little Andrei grew curious about all the noise and excitement over there, pleading with his parents to take him to a game until his father broke down and bought some tickets. Bored, Tzelikovsky *père* went back to the apartment after the second inning, but his son remained seated, watching in wide-eyed wonder until the last out. The experience turned him into a rabid Expos fan, and he followed them on TV, collecting baseball books and magazines and even a few instructional videos, which he watched again and again on his VCR.

When the Tzelikovskys returned to Moscow, Andrei reentered the volleyball academy, but his heart wasn't in it anymore. (Every time he says the words *Red Army*, he makes a face, as if he'd just been served a plate of month-old cabbage.) He no longer dreamed of being famous for spiking shots over a net; instead, he wanted to be a baseball player. There were no diamonds anywhere in the city, though, so he practiced at a neighborhood park every Sunday, using a stick and a tennis ball to give his friends batting instruction. He did not touch a real bat in Russia until he went out for the Olympic team.

His memories of the training camp are still vivid, in fact. The scene was chaotic, he says, at least in the early days, with dozens of fit-looking, well-intentioned Soviet men gripping baseballs and pegging them to one another, often missing their intended target by more than a yard. Still, out of the chaos a number of promising athletes emerged, and they formed the nucleus of the Red Devils: four tennis players, an Olympic medallist in handball, Tzelikovsky himself, and three former javelin throwers, who gave up factory jobs to become pitchers.

"It was difficult at first," Tzelikovsky told me, tugging at the bill of his red cap, which had the letters CCCP stitched in gold across its crown. "Our equipment was not very good. We just had some old stuff that Cuban players had left behind. Our own players didn't know the rules. Sometimes, if they hit the ball they ran to third base instead of to first. And our Soviet umpires didn't know the rules, either. They made them up for their own pleasure. How could we argue with them? The first game we ever played, we lost 48–0, to a visiting team from Nicaragua. We needed coaching very badly. One afternoon on the metro, I was riding home from a game in my uniform, and an American, a student, came up to me. He had pitched for Colgate University—do you know about Colgate?—so I asked him to come out and teach us about curveballs." Tzelikovsky paused to shrug. "In this way," he said, "we began to improve."

When the Red Devils were still down by twenty-one runs in the middle of the seventh inning, the various coaches, umpires, factotums, and functionaries in attendance at Diablo Valley reached a wise and probably merciful decision, relying on some English and some sign language, to call the game. There was a little daylight left, so the Soviet players took advantage of it by retreating to the batting cages and laboring at their hitting until dusk, pointing up how disciplined and hardworking they are. If you're a Red Devil, you don't want to miss a practice session unless you have a good excuse. Alexei Pavlinchuk, the team's manager, a Sverdlovsk native with penetrating eyes, runs a tight ship and doles out fines with abandon. Anyone caught drinking without permission loses half his salary for the month. Smoking without permission is also frowned on, and costs the perpetrator a fourth of his salary. If you curse, you pay ten rubles for the first offense and double that for the second. There is no appeal.

While the Red Devils were taking their cuts, I sat in the stands with Tim Hickerson, who was responsible for bringing the Soviet team to California. A former minor leaguer in the Chicago Cubs system, Hickerson is an intelligent, soft-spoken man in his mid-thirties who loves baseball as much as Andrei Tzelikovsky does. As the proprietor of a fledgling travel agency in San Francisco, he arranges vacations abroad for American amateurs who want to play against foreign teams in their natural habitat, and does the same sort of thing for foreign teams that want to come to the United States. The Red Devils were involved in such an exchange program. Hickerson had sent a team from Monte Vista High School, in Danville, near San Ramon, on a ten-day trip to Moscow, and now a boosters' group from Monte Vista was reciprocating by hosting the Soviets, providing them with complimentary lodging and meals along with their airfare.

The Red Devils' next game was in Stockton, at Delta Junior College, and when Hickerson offered me a ride to the ballpark I accepted. He picked me up at the Marriott in a beat-up Chevy Nova, cream-colored, whose odometer had rolled over at least once. The car made odd sounds. It did not inspire confidence. But Hickerson, who sometimes drives a cab to stay afloat, appeared to be in control of the vehicle. Although he isn't in playing condition anymore, he still has an athlete's reflexes. He was an All-Conference center fielder during his university days, at Berkeley—Jackie Jensen recruited him—but he's built more like a catcher, thick through the chest and stubby in the legs. I mentioned this to him, and he said that he used to be taller, but he'd fallen off a roof while working as a roofer eleven years ago and had shrunk a little.

As an exercise, I once scribbled out a list of all the jobs Hickerson has held. It read like an author's bio from the he-man epoch of American literature, when no dust jacket was complete without a catalog of unpredictable employ-ment. In addition to being a roofer, he'd been a logger, an usher at a theater, a reporter for the *People's Daily World*, a baseball manager in the Italian major leagues, the stage manager for a travelling French magician, and a batting coach in Managua. Then, too, you had to take his aspira-tions into account. He had wanted to act, to direct films, and also to be a writer in the way of Hemingway or Henry Miller, all to no avail.

We had spectacular weather for our trip to Stockton. The night before, an Alaskan storm had blown through California, leaving the green hills of the East Bay dusted with snow. Creeks that had been dead dry a month ago were running high and muddy, spilling over rocks and flow-ing down past black oaks and pepper trees. There was a sweet fragrance in the air, and I found myself thinking about Andrei Tzelikovsky, who would already be at the ball-park, dressed in his uniform and eager for action.

Hickerson was daydreaming about baseball, too. It's his central obsession, and he said that if his travel business clicks he hopes to coach or play in Japan or Australia, or maybe in Cuba—anywhere, really, that he can get a game. He has already played in Moscow, having gone there with a team of over-the-hill baseball lovers, among them an attorney, a doctor, and a psychologist. For the privilege of engaging the Red Devils on their home turf, the American wannabes paid Hickerson about three thousand dollars apiece. Hickerson had been to the Soviet Union before, so he informed his charges that they were in for culture shock, not a Club Med holiday. They should expect sterile rooms, flimsy towels, rough toilet paper, and lots of cheese, sausage, caviar, and heavy brown bread.

If Hickerson has any regrets about his devotion to baseball, they focus on his failure to make the big leagues. After leaving Berkeley, he played with the Bradenton Cubs in the Florida rookie league and did well enough to be asked to the Cubs' instructional-league camp that fall. When he hit .349 in a forty-game season, he was sure that he'd be offered a AAA contract. Instead, the Cubs sent him a contract similar to the one he'd had in the rookie league. He accepted the contract very reluctantly, and when he went to Arizona for spring training, he had some run-ins with the Cubs front office and was dropped from the squad. He figured that on the basis of his hitting another team would want him, but he was turned down everywhere. He handled the dismissal poorly and became a little lost and purposeless until, through the intercession of a baseball pal from Berkeley, he landed a manager's job in San Giovanni in Persiceto, Italy.

Hickerson had never heard of San Giovanni in Persiceto, but he learned that it was a city of about twenty thousand, not far from Bologna. He lived in one room at the Hotel Leone and earned about five hundred dollars a month for directing a team of semi-pros, who played their games on weekends. Of necessity he became fluent in Italian. He loved Italian food, women, and wine, and made many friends. In the off-season, when there wasn't any baseball, he sometimes stayed in San Giovanni anyway and supported himself by giving English lessons.

In all, he managed five different Italian clubs over the next few years. The players he dealt with could be peculiarly challenging in their demands. Hickerson once had an American transplant who wouldn't practice unless he could get bacon and eggs at a trattoria every morning. He had an outfielder who tried to catch fly balls by holding his mitt stationary in front of his face. He had a pitcher who declined to issue intentional walks, because they reflected badly on his masculinity.

"After my first season at San Giovanni, I went back to California for a couple of years and then took a job in

Castenaso," he told me, flipping on his directional signal as we approached Stockton. "I got fired for arguing with the team's owner. I thought that was it for Italy, so I went home again, but then I changed my mind and came back for one more try. Nobody hired me, though, and by the summer I was sitting around in San Giovanni with a bottle of whiskey and a plane ticket to the United States. But on the day I was going to leave I got a message that the *presidente* of the Sant'Arcangelo di Romagna club was coming to see me. He pulled up in a huge Peugeot sedan. He was a big, fat guy, maybe three hundred pounds, whose passion was collecting stamps. He asked me to take over Sant'Arcangelo for the second half of the season, and gave me a car, an apartment, and even a washing machine.

"I had a great success and turned the team from losers into winners. We were based near Rimini, and we used to drink Chianti and swim in the Adriatic to celebrate our victories. The Florence Lions, one of Italy's top teams, hired me away from Sant'Arcangelo, but they expected a miracle from me, and when I didn't deliver it they fired me. After that, the only club that wanted me was Godo. Do you know Godo?" I said that I didn't, and Hickerson said, "Godo is in the second division."

The two oldest players on the Red Devils, Leonid Korneyev and German Gulbitt—thirty-four and thirty-six, respectively—are pitchers, although Korneyev, who carries a big bat, doubles as a first baseman. By virtue of their maturity, they seemed to be enjoying the tour more than the younger players, not taking things quite so seriously. At the Marriott one night, Gulbitt approached me dressed in an incredible suit with inch-wide gray and white stripes and tried to sell me a Soviet watch. When I said *"Nyet,"* politely and with a grin, Gulbitt reacted merrily, as if we were just messing around, and gave me a gentle little pat on the back before continuing to work his way through the potential customers in the hotel lobby.

Korneyev happened to be on the mound at Delta Junior College when Hickerson and I arrived. Heavyset and powerful-looking, he throws hard for a Red Devil, and the Mustangs of Delta were having difficulty timing his pitches. To the amazement of practically everyone, the score was tied at 3—all in the bottom of the third inning. The ballpark at the college was really very pretty and well maintained, and that might have contributed to the Red Devils' improving their game. There were dugouts and new bleachers, the grass had recently been cut, and an outfield wall (a row of tall bushes behind a chain-link fence) bound all the elements together in a sweet symmetry. A decent crowd had turned out, too, more than a hundred people, and everyone would laugh good-naturedly when, say, Alexander Krupenchenkov came to bat and a student announcer on the P.A. system tried to wrap his tongue around the unfamiliar syllables.

Stockton has always had a reputation as a conservative city, so it surprised me when the fans applauded the Soviet players for making a nice catch or stealing a base, but Hickerson told me he'd observed this phenomenon every time he'd seen the Red Devils compete in the United States. Apparently, Americans were touched by their earnestness and wanted them to know they were appreciated. As we sat watching the game, another thing that Hickerson had said resonated in my mind—that because the Red Devils had learned their baseball as adults, their movements on the field seemed slightly unnatural. For instance, although they threw with marvelous accuracy, there was usually a noticeable hitch, or a slight pause, *before* the throw, which indicated that a thought had preceded the action. The smooth, silky quality of intuition that sends a shortstop gliding toward the hole in advance of a ball's being hit there was missing from their play.

The Red Devils were also lacking in infield chatter. A kind of loose-limbed, high-spirited jive runs through an American team when it's humming, but the Soviets were not yet comfortable enough on a baseball diamond to relax. Sometimes they were as studiously correct as pupils at a dancing school, concentrating so hard on their steps that they scarcely heard the melody. The word "fun" was not a constant in their vocabulary. But, on the other hand, they were still in the early stages of their evolution, and had only just reached the point where they were starting to invent some baseball slang. They called the diamond, in Russian, "the square." A pop fly was a "candle." If a player made a sharp, precise throw, someone might say, "Sergei, that was a real bayonet!" The area where the infield dirt gives way to the crescent-shaped outfield grass was known as "the moon," and this allowed the Red Devils to indulge a lyrical impulse by saying, when Tzelikovsky trotted to his position, "Andrei has gone to the moon."

Like most forcibly retired baseball managers, Hickerson has trouble attending a game without voicing his opinions. At Stockton, he kept second-guessing Pavlinchuk. Doubtless Hickerson would have liked to don a Red Devils uniform and assume the managerial helm. Although his Russian was limited to a few phrases, he knew some of the Soviet players by name and had conversed with them both here and abroad, often through an interpreter. If a ballplayer asked him for some batting tips, he was glad to oblige.

Unfortunately for the Red Devils, the tide began to turn in the fifth inning. They stayed in contention, tying the score again at 5–all, but the Mustangs had the home-field advantage, and they chipped away at the Soviet pitchers and went on to win by four runs. This was the closest the Red Devils had ever come to a victory in California, but they still didn't look very happy. They weren't fond of losing to Americans. They had a diplomatic attitude about it, though, and immediately embarked on their postgame ritual, emptying their duffelbags and displaying the goods that they'd brought along to barter.

The Mustangs stepped tentatively forward and fingered the clothing, as they might at a flea market. Yevgeny Puchkov (.444 average last year) had a deal going with one Mustang, who wanted to trade an old mitt for something Russian. Along with generating some slang, the Red Devils are acquiring nicknames, and Puchkov, who has a brooding countenance, is known as Mubarak, because he resembles the Egyptian President. Infielder Ilya Bogatirev picked up the moniker Home Boy on the team's last American swing, while Alexander Vidyaev, a second baseman, must toil under the weight of a Russian diminutive—Malenky (Little One)—which, though it's endearing, he hates.

"You got any of those funky fur hats?" the Mustang asked. "That's what I really want to trade you for."

Puchkov examined the mitt on offer, which was streaked and pitted and begrimed and had turned a skunky shade of blackish brown. "No hats," he said, before reaching into his bag and pulling out a tank top that showed a cartoonish Gorby and several apparatchiks astride Harley-Davidson motorcycles. The legend beneath the illustration, done in heavy-metal style, read "KREMLIN CREW." Gorby had the middle finger of one hand extended.

The tank top made the Mustang giggle. "No way I want that," he protested. "I want one of them fur hats."

"No hats," Puchov informed him again, shaking his head wearily, as if the Mustang had overlooked a tremendous bargain.

Every dedicated ballplayer keeps a mental record of how he's doing, and when fans asked Andrei Tzelikovsky for a rundown of his stats after the Delta Junior College game, he said, "I am three for nine at the plate. I have made no fielding errors." That was a satisfactory performance, he felt, although not exactly thrilling. Tzelikovsky wished that he had the uncanny grace of his batting hero, Ted Williams, whose book *The Science of Hitting* he'd read more than twenty times. Once, while we were hanging out, I brought up a famous story about Williams' eyesight, which was supposed to be so sharp that he could see, in minute particulars, his bat making contact with the ball.

"Ya, ya, I know," Tzelikovsky said. He told me that he hoped Pavlinchuk might let him pitch an inning or two before the tour was over. He had pitched in Moscow, he said, and a radar gun had clocked his fastball at seventy-eight miles per hour.

On his free afternoons, Tzelikovsky had been joining his teammates on field trips coordinated by the Red Devils' hosts in San Ramon. The players went to Chinatown in San Francisco, and they were bused to various suburban malls and invited to do some browsing. This put them in a bit of a fix, since they had only a little ready cash, but they learned to bypass Macy's and Nordstrom and head for dis-count stores like Kmart, where, at rock-bottom prices, they bought fanny packs, Walkman knock-offs, and cheap sets of carving knives.

When there were no special activities planned, Tze-likovsky liked to stay in his room at the hotel. He relished the spaciousness and the privacy, and watched ballgames and movies on TV. At his executive-style desk, he wrote postcards to his friends and family. An only child, he still lived with his mother and father, even though they were disappointed in him for dropping volleyball (and the safety of a career in the Red Army) for the iffiness of Soviet base-ball. Out of his salary, he contributed fifty rubles a month toward household expenses. The Tzelikovskys were feeling a financial pinch these days, like most other Russians, he said. The shelves in Moscow's food stores were frequently empty, and the lines of customers were long.

As an antidote to all this, Tzelikovsky made it a point to treat himself to lunch every afternoon at the McDonald's in Red Square—it was his only luxury. In his scrupulous way, he'd been comparing the McDonald's cuisine in the Bay Area with the franchised food at home. The burgers tasted the same, he submitted, but in the milkshakes he detected subtle differences.

He enjoyed telling me about the famous baseball players he'd met, too. In Baltimore once, he had spent time with Mark McGwire and picked up some pointers, while in

Moscow fate had led him to an encounter with Sadaharu Oh, Japan's greatest slugger and a figure of near-mythological proportions. Tzelikovsky watched Oh give a batting demonstration and then—better yet—had an opportunity to speak with him and get some Zen-like advice.

"Baseball is cooperation, not competition," Oh instructed him. "A pitcher is your friend, not your enemy. He is sending you a gift, and it is your responsibility as a batter to send it right back to him, toward the bleachers."

One night at the end of the Red Devils' tour, Tzelikovsky had to go to San Francisco for a radio interview, and we decided to ride in together with Tim Hickerson as our chauffeur. Waiting in the hotel lobby for the guest of honor to finish his shower, Hickerson looked ill at ease in the presence of so much marble and glitter. In his current economic state, an Italian meal at a North Beach restaurant amounted to a splurge, he confessed. But Hickerson felt no ambivalence about starting a new business at a time in life when some of his contemporaries were already looking forward to retiring. "I like travelling," he said happily. "I like Russians. I like being in uniform and chewing tobacco. I like bullshitting. Hey, I get to be a little boy again!"

When Tzelikovsky swept into the lobby, clean and neat in his best clothes, we piled into the Nova and took off for the city. Tzelikovsky showed no signs of nervousness. He assured us that he'd been on the radio before, and once he was in front of a microphone at KSFO-AM, he proved to be in his element, nimbly fielding questions from callers.

"Hiya, Andrei. I was just wondering, you admire any American players?"

"Ya. Here are three—Lenny Dykstra, Bob Welch, and Mark McGwire. I met Mark McGwire in Baltimore. I have a letter he wrote to me in Moscow."

"Is he a good guy?"

"Ya."

"Andrei, how do you keep up with baseball when you're over there in Russia?"

"It's difficult. I listen to Voice of America for the scores."

"Yo, Andrei. It's cool you're here in California, man. What do you think about Rickey Henderson? He's making, like—what?—three million dollars?"

"Rickey is worth it."

"You really think that?"

"Rickey is worth every penny."

After the interview, Tzelikovsky wanted to peek into the Hard Rock Cafe. (One T-shirt that the Red Devils were selling had the restaurant's emblem on it, with the words "Hard Rock" in Cyrillic.) While Hickerson idled at the curb, I led Tzelikovsky through the door and into a dining room decked out with electric guitars, Elvis photos, gold records, and other rock-and-roll memorabilia. The place must have appeared unimaginably bright and wealthy to Tzelikovsky, but he didn't seem to be impressed, and said as we left that he had always thought it was a *private* club. Then we parked at a McDonald's and bought him a dinner of a Big Mac, fries, some kind of pie-like thing, and a chocolate milkshake, all to go.

And then we were on the freeway again, returning to San Ramon. It was a moonless night, and we drove through a landscape of farms, ranches, and weedy fields mixed in with new suburbs and industrial parks. On the radio, Tzelikovsky had been careful not to say anything critical of the United States, so I asked him to tell me, in all honesty, if there was anything about the country that he didn't like. He meditated for a minute and said, "The people here live very far from one another." He said it soberly. After that, we changed the subject to baseball, and Tzelikovsky spoke of his eagerness for the U.S.S.R. season to begin. The Soviet first division was going to expand to ten teams, so the Red Devils would play fifty-four games, not just twenty-eight. There were supposed to be teams in Kiev, Vladivostok, Odessa, and Tbilisi. At the mention of Tbilisi, Hickerson got excited and said, "Tbilisi? I'd love to play in Georgia!"

In the morning, the Red Devils had a game with the Monte Vista High School team. The weather did them a favor this time, turning cool and blustery and reminding them of Moscow. Tzelikovsky was in a batting cage practicing his swing when I got there, and after he finished we talked by the dugout. He proudly showed me his most recent American purchase—a plaque with Mark McGwire's picture on it, which he had bartered for at a sporting-goods store. But he soon became gloomy and serious again, and told me that he hadn't yet bought any gifts for his parents, because he had no money left. It occurred to me that it might not be a bad thing to own a nesting doll, so we haggled over the one Andrei had in his duffelbag and settled on a price of twenty dollars. When I gave him the bill, he folded it in quarters, stuck it in a pocket, shook hands with me, and said, in his grave manner, "Thank you very much." He tapped the dirt from his spikes after that, adjusted his cap, and ran briskly toward the outfield, going to the moon.

5
The Quarter Pole

THEY WERE COMING across the Acadian prairie from a long way off, men in battered pickup trucks hauling their horse trailers past the corn and the soybeans, the rice and the sugarcane. Already the temperature was in the nineties, but the men refused to pay the heat any mind. They were weekend trainers from Carencro and Lake Charles, Lafayette and Abbeville, and instead they'd be busy thinking up clever, devious, or downright crooked strategies to win a few dollars in purse money at the Quarter Pole, the last bush track in Louisiana and probably on the planet.

Rayne, it should be noted, is the Frog Capital of the United States. I discovered that weird factoid on the day I drove into town. More frogs are plucked from its bayous than anywhere else in the country, and whenever frogs are scarce, the local restaurants import some from Indonesia. The Cajun way to serve frog legs is deep-fried, but I had acquired a taste for mine sautéed in butter and garlic. And at dinner every night, I liked to begin with an appetizer of grilled alligator sausages—chewy, spicy, and served with puffy white bread for sopping up the juices.

The low-down food was a side issue for me, in reality. I was in Rayne to watch a bush race or two before the sport vanished forever. Bush tracks are a breeding ground for mayhem, and they used to be found wherever Cajun people lived. The old-timers love to carry on about the epic match races of yore, when two quarter horses knocked heads for boasting rights and pots as high as $50,000. Since my arrival, I had heard tales of colts doped up on cocaine and morphine, owners who could be swayed by the puniest bribe, and betting coups that made rich men out of hay balers, shrimpers, and sad-assed roustabouts.

Things have changed since the glory days in the thirties and forties, of course, but the Quarter Pole is still a rakish spot that old Huey Long, the Kingfish, would have relished. Every aspect of the operation is fluid and open to conjecture. There are no vets, stewards, or officials on the premises, for instance. Horses aren't examined before they run a race, nor are they tested after it. The only judge on the grounds occupies a lawn chair near the finish line. The jockeys weigh in on a bathroom scale and ride in their street clothes. As for the track, it's a ratty mile-long oval as hard as a cast-iron skillet.

The Quarter Pole is a dicey place, then, but the weekend trainers keep showing up, anyway—guys like Donny Jones from Baton Rouge, who was the first to pull into the parking lot that Sunday. Jones wore a Yankees cap, had a gold front tooth, and looked as if he belonged in a hip-hop group. With some difficulty, he coaxed a gelding from his trailer, a two-year-old maiden named Big Money—optimism incarnate! The horse would run in the fifth race, against two other maidens. For the privilege of competing, Jones had to pay an entry fee of $15. If Big Money won, he'd sweep the $45 purse, although he could earn a lot more on side bets, depending on what sort of tricks he had up his sleeve.

Big Money was very green and behaved so rankly that he spooked Jones' designated rider, an undernourished guy in black trousers that were shiny in the seat. "Say now!" the rider cried, jumping back from the flying hooves. "Don't be shooting your feet out at me!"

"Be nice to the horse," Jones advised him.

The rider frowned. He thought for a second, then rushed up and gave Big Money a swift kick in the flank. "Now we're even!" he shouted.

Jones shrugged and led Big Money toward the Quarter Pole's tottery old receiving barn. The gelding was limping, favoring a tender leg.

I observed this melodrama from the distance, while I was talking with Joseph Abshire, or Mr. Joe, as he's known in Acadia Parish. Mr. Joe was briefing me on how he'd once played fiddle in a band with four of his eight brothers—Little Joe and the Southern Gentlemen, they were called. They caroused in juke joints until the wee hours, then woke at dawn to labor in the rice fields for $20 a month. It should come as no surprise that Mr. Joe saw no future in fieldwork, so he diversified and became a successful building contractor. With his wife, Virginia, he raised four children, including two daughters born in the same year, but it was his only son, Clifford, who had convinced him to buy the Quarter Pole for $360,000.

Cliff Abshire, at forty-five, doesn't take after his old man. Where Mr. Joe is abrupt and literal, Cliff is a drowsy-eyed dreamer. When I first met him, he seemed half-asleep, but he does perk up whenever a pretty woman is around. He views himself as the Casanova of the Quarter Pole and lives in a funky trailer off the backstretch that doesn't commend itself to drop-in visits. He used to run jumbo shrimp from New Iberia to Texas, where he could score a higher price, and has also worked at various quarter horse tracks around the South. Once, he explained to me all the ways a bush race can be doctored—too many to list, in fact.

I asked Cliff to give me a tour of the Quarter Pole before the races began, and he was glad to oblige.

"See that pond?" he crowed, gesturing toward an algae-choked puddle in the infield. "They's alligators in there, son. Anybody falls in, he's sure to be eaten."

Next, he led me into the receiving barn and down a dusty shed row to the stalls where he stables four horses of his own. "This here is Mister Fugly," he said, showing me a tired bay with far too many miles on him. "That's short for mother-effin' ugly." He balled up a fist and punched Mister Fugly in the jaw. Mister Fugly hardly blinked, so familiar was the treatment.

Farther down the shed row, a sorry-looking fellow named Ed was sponging off an arthritic thoroughbred. The horse's most recent claim to fame was that he had finished last in a race at Evangeline Downs, outside Lafayette, the night before.

"He truly so bad, to be dead last?" Cliff wanted to know.

"Yeah, he's that bad," Ed said. "But at least he had it in him to run until the end."

"Well, that's the main thing." Cliff cupped a Marlboro in his palm and launched into a recurrent fantasy about how the Quarter Pole would make a great location for a movie, in a more blessed future. "We could get Chuck Norris to star in it," he went on. "I met him at Evangeline once. He's just a little-bitty man, you know? I doubt he weighs more than 130, 135 pounds."

"He really so little and small?" Ed asked.

"Yeah, he is. When we fix up the plant here, maybe I'll invite him by." This was another of Cliff's fantasies. He had a vision of how splendid the Quarter Pole would look once it was repaired, renovated, and remodeled. He had even gotten an estimate of the cost—about $1.5 million. Where the money would come from was anybody's guess, but Cliff believed an investor would fall out of the clouds someday, in the way of a TV angel descending from heaven. When that happened, he said, the Abshires would have simulcast wagering and be a tourist attraction on a par with Bourbon Street in New Orleans.

By mid-morning, the sun was fiery in a cloudless sky. I broke a sweat walking over to the receiving barn, where Donny Jones and some other trainers were tending to their stock. While a tape deck poured out country stomp, the trainers wrapped faulty legs in bandages, administered medication to animals in need, swallowed aspirin themselves, and swapped war stories about their woes. They were at the Quarter Pole for the fun of it, really, and also because they loved their horses, even though the horses, in most cases, had done nothing to merit being loved.

William Duplichan, an oil-truck driver, was typical of the weekenders. He felt on intimate terms with bad luck and cast a critical eye on Streakin Chip Chip, his lone entry, who was padding about in a stall.

"That horse," Duplichan told me glumly, "he won the very first time he run. He won at a recognized track, too, but he ain't won since, and he's had seven chances. Seven chances! Trouble is, he's scared of everything. He spooks, and he don't break from the gate at all. But he can be fast, I *guar-ran-tree*. I'm going to sell him as a saddle horse. You think he might be worth fifteen hundred dollars?"

"Might could be," another trainer allowed. "You never know."

"No, you don't know. But maybe he's only worth a thousand."

"You never know."

"No, sir, you don't." Duplichan glanced around and counted heads. "Where are all the jockeys at? Hey, I'll tell you what. There won't *be* enough jockeys here today!"

A couple of fans drifted into the barn, two men clutching cold cans of beer. They were wiry Cajuns in straw Stetsons, who'd paid three dollars to get in; women paid only a dollar for the pleasure of being fleeced, and kids fended for themselves. The men had free programs stuffed into their back pockets—a single sheet that listed the horses running in all six races, as well as the owner and trainer of each (often the same person), but not much else. Handicapping was impossible at the Quarter Pole, given the absence of reliable information, so the search for hot tips was ceaseless.

"Your horse in number five race, he look good?" one of the fans asked.

"He looked good earlier," a trainer told him sourly. "But he don't look good now."

"Maybe he needs a nap."

"He ain't going to get it."

Hovering close to the barn, too, were Joseph Meaux and Kevin DeVille, a pair of hard-nosed young men who galloped horses in the morning for the sheer thrill of it. They dipped snuff and spat with authority, and their fondest wish was to be licensed jockeys, like Joseph's father, Claude, but they hadn't quite figured out how to go about it and were in an intense, unsteady competition as to who would accomplish the feat first.

When I complained to them about the humidity, DeVille chuckled and said, "This heat is fine! My hands don't work right in the cold."

"Cold don't bother me," Meaux countered, dribbling out some brown spit. "I go on winter trail rides."

"So do I," DeVille said quickly. "I ride trail in the winter *all* the time. I ride through the lightning!" He was really cooking now. "I ride through the *thunderstorms*!"

"The thunderstorms?" Meaux asked.

"I ride to meet my *mother*!"

That was too much poetry for me, so I wandered over to the grandstand and stopped at the bar for a beer. Every stool was occupied, and the cans were being emptied at a furious pace. In a kitchen in back, Virginia Abshire was putting the crowning touches on her jambalaya—a bargain at $2.50 a plate. She'd had her hair done for the races, and offered me her recipe for gumbo, secret as it might have been.

"The chicken goes in first, without a doubt," she said firmly. "After two hours, you add the sausage and let the gumbo simmer for ten minutes. The number one ticket is green onion tops, and you got to have a serious roux."

"Take pride in your cooking!" Cliff yelled from his stool.

"That's right," his mother said. "Dare to be better than anybody else!"

Dianna Abshire, Cliff's sister, was the busiest family member around. She was the track's accountant, gardener, barmaid, and racing secretary. It was her responsibility to draw up the card, too. Trainers phoned her with their entries on Saturday afternoon, and she had the program typed and copied by Sunday morning. The trainers could be finicky, she said, and they always picked their spots with care, avoiding any enemies. There were deep rivalries and blood feuds among Acadian Cajuns that could be traced back to the primal mists.

"The only thing I knew about racing before this," Dianna said, "was to sit down in my seat and have a good time. Now I don't have a minute to myself, with so much to do and not enough help from the family." She stared pointedly at Cliff. "But our races are something else! We've raced mules here, and even Shetland ponies. Once, six men put up thirty dollars apiece, climbed into the starting gate, and ran a footrace, winner take all. Us women wanted to race the same way—and we would have!—but I realized if we did, there wouldn't be anybody left to do the work."

Rising from his bar stool, Cliff Abshire prepared to tackle his only formal job at the Quarter Pole. As the track announcer, glib and ever hoping to charm, he commanded a table near the bar, propped up his feet, and drawled into a microphone over a scratchy public-address system. His voice was sly and oily, even though the first bulletin he delivered wasn't what the crowd cared to hear.

"Folks, looks like we won't be startin' at one o'clock, after all," he said, making a show of consulting his watch. "We're runnin' a little behind schedule. Seems this one jockey, his car broke down on the prairie, but he fixed it, and he's on his way comin' here. Be about, oh, twenty minutes."

The fans waiting by the paddock howled and groaned. The temperature was over a hundred now, and they'd been socking down beer for three hours or so, not counting the beer they might have drunk at breakfast. When thirty minutes went by without the jockey reporting for duty, their howling reached a fever pitch. I thought a revolution was imminent, with Cliff being rousted from his regal perch and fed to the infield alligators piece by piece, but he must have sensed it, because he pleaded for a substitute rider—no experience necessary—and when a volunteer raised a hand we were ready to start at last.

I watched all three trainers lead their thoroughbreds into the paddock. It's an old joke, but I counted the horses' legs.

"I get the feeling!" a tattooed man next to me roared. The sleeves of his T-shirt were rolled up to his shoulders and showed off his massive biceps, as forceful as Aaron Neville's. "Twenty dollars on the Two!"

That's how the wagering goes on at the Quarter Pole. With no tote board or pari-mutuel windows, it's one person betting against another. The lack of data on the horses encourages absurd hunches, wild ideas, and plain old stabs in the dark. Ordinarily, the tattooed man would find a taker, but Shot Byruff, the Two, looked so much healthier than Beau Fly and Phar Lap that he was a clear favorite.

"I get the feeling!" the tattooed man roared again, becoming agitated. He spun on a heel to confront another fan, who leaned on a cane and had a shaved and burnished head. "Hey, you there! You, baldie! Why you don't square with me on the Three or the One?"

Baldie gaped in disbelief. "What you think I am, *cher*?" he asked grandly, playing to his audience. "Am I just off a banana boat from some tropical island? Am I some type of really stupid fool? No, my friend. I assure you, I am an African-American *gentleman*!"

The tattooed man said, "We all the same here, brother."

"We are not the same!"

Those banalities were tossed back and forth a few times, until Baldie lost control, lifted his cane, and aimed a blow at his oppressor's skull. He missed, fortunately, but I still thought I'd live to see a trail of teeth and bones strewn around the paddock. It might have happened, too, if some strong-arm boys hadn't broken up the quarrel. As tempers cooled, the odds on a full-scale race riot dropped from even money to 10-to-1, and the races finally began.

The jockeys, including the volunteer, saddled up and nudged their mounts onto the track. After a short warm-up, they entered the starting gate for a four-and-a-half-furlong sprint. The horses stood calmly, but when the rusty gate snapped open, Phar Lap reared up and threw his rider—the same belligerent guy who'd kicked Big Money! Could karma be operating at the Quarter Pole? I wondered. While the rider lay in the dirt, Phar Lap turned tail and galloped off in the wrong direction. For a minute, it looked as if Phar Lap would collide with the other horses, but the tattooed man, of all possible benefactors, leaped over the rail and flagged down the runaway.

I had expected strange doings in Rayne, and my expectations were being met. As for the downed rider, he was on his feet again and accepting advice from well-wishers, who urged him to breathe deeply, loosen his trousers, drink cold water, drink hot water, and rest in the shade. It was all too much for him, though, and he fainted. It struck me that he might be dead, but he blinked twice while he was flat on his back and moaned, "Help me up, folks. I got three more horses to ride." Ride them he did. They were all losers.

Now the quarter horses took center stage. Cliff Abshire read off their names before each race, but he spent most of his energy slipping double entendres to a slinky, blue-jeaned blond, who appeared to be both flattered and disgusted. He grabbed me once and said, "Go on down there and tell her I own this racetrack," and when I refused he made a face, cussed at me, and dragged in a flunky to do his bidding.

In the third race, Streakin Chip Chip had another chance to redeem himself, but he performed just as Duplichan predicted, departing from the gate long after the other horses. It was certain that children might soon be riding Streakin

Chip Chip at carnivals and church bazaars. Donny Jones fared a little better, although not as well as he might have liked. Big Money did fine in the gate, but the horse couldn't keep up with Cajun Jet, a heavily bet Rayne celebrity, and cost Jones his $15.

I watched the race with Cowboy Meaux, Joseph's grandfather, and a security guard, who had long since forgotten about the concept of security. The Cowboy saw that Big Money was a gelding and told how he had once gelded a colt by himself in his days as a groom. It required some sharp instruments and a fifth of Jack Daniel's, he said, plus the colt proved to have three testicles.

"He have three balls for real?" the guard asked, dumbfounded.

"Damn straight," Cowboy swore. "And he ran much better without 'em."

By the sixth and last race, I recognized an expression of despair on the faces of some fans. They were having no luck, and since luck is all that matters when you bet on bush racing, where every variable is fluid, they were in trouble. Every Cajun knows that luck can't be courted. Instead, it's sprinkled randomly around the universe, landing on a rice grower one afternoon and his bluetick hound the next. All a person can do when confronted with such chaos is give up and toss a party—which the fans proceeded to do, cranking up the jukebox in the bar and doing the two-step to a medley of Hank Williams tunes.

The party was loud, ornery, and in full swing when I got ready to leave. Some trainers were loading their trailers again for the drive back to everyday routine—wives, kids, mortgages, and bosses—but others moved straight to the bar and would stay there until closing time at 2 A.M. Cliff was at his usual spot, too, shooting a game of eight-ball and showing off the phone number he'd got from the slinky blond. We all cherish our triumphs, of course, and I believed my trip to the Quarter Pole was one, with the track living up to its madcap reputation, so I planned to reward myself with some alligator sausage and frog legs at Sweet P's in town, before I headed home.

6
In Prime Time

CITIES OFTEN RUN on a fuel of power, money, and ego, but sometimes they can run on pure hype, as Atlantic City, New Jersey, did in the days before Mike Tyson fought Michael Spinks for the undisputed heavyweight championship of the world. The man responsible for the bout was Donald Trump, who owned two profitable casinos in town and was constructing a third, modestly called the Taj Mahal. Trump appears to be in love with certain slick catchwords, including *plaza, success,* and *celebrity,* and he'd probably stamp his name on clouds and mountains if anybody gave him a ch·nce.

For the right to host the Tyson-Spinks extravaganza, Trump coughed up eleven million dollars to the promoters, outbidding several tyros in Las Vegas. That sounds like a bold stroke, in line with his real-estate grabs, but he actually had little to lose. Trump understands Americans and shares their passion for statistics, for size and volume, for sheer mass in preference to anything abstract or foreign. A heavyweight title match carries with it a huge freight of expectations, and people anywhere near one tend to go crazy and throw their money away at the gaming tables whether their favorite wins or loses. But even if the fans chose to sit on their cash, Trump stood to recoup his investment just by selling tickets to the fight.

To a developer like Trump, Mike Tyson must have resembled the human equivalent of a bulldozer. I was in awe of his prowess myself and had made it my business to be on hand when the chips were down. I'd followed Tyson from the start of his career, watching Cus D'Amato, his original trainer, bring him along slowly and build him up on a steady diet of tomato cans—lumpy guys Iron Mike disposed of in a round or two—until he was ready, at the age of twenty, to take the WBC belt from Trevor Berbick and become the youngest heavyweight champ in history. (Spinks owned the IBF belt.) Tyson's ferocity impressed me, too. When he hit other boxers, he raised ugly, hive-like welts on their skin—Tysonitis, the pundits called it. If he pounded on your arms for six minutes, you couldn't lift them anymore; after nine minutes, you wished the arms would fall off.

Aside from his purely physical gifts, Tyson was dangerous because of his temper. A member of his camp told me once that he loses control at times and goes bananas, banging on the walls and throwing around the furniture, but he can also be kind, funny, and playful. He speaks with a slight

lisp—his childhood nickname was Fairy Boy—and appears
to be sensitive, intelligent, and emotionally complex. Those
qualities didn't do him any good while he was growing up
in a debilitating Brooklyn slum, so he hid them behind a
warrior's mask and went about his muggings and robberies
with a feral, untroubled glee. His violent nature still comes
out in the ring, and it's frightening to see. It grips him like
a ghostly possession and pushes him over the edge, into a
no-man's-land where the usual rules don't apply.

In Atlantic City, there may have been nobody as scared
of Tyson as Michael Spinks, who spoke openly of his distaste for boxing and admitted that he was only in it for the
payday. Ten years older than his opponent, Spinks was a
sweet-natured man—an all-night dancer, a fancier of stylish hats and clothes—whose life had been riddled with
tragedies. His common-law wife died in a car crash, leaving
him a daughter he dotes on, and he had almost lost his
brother Leon to the fight game many times. Once the
champ himself, a conqueror of the great Muhammed Ali,
Leon blew his earnings on drugs and had problems with
the law. Despite Michael's financial support, he accepted
fights in cow towns and got beat up for peanuts. Then his
brother had to chase after him and rescue him again.

So in Leon, Michael might well have seen a premoni-
tion of what he might become himself if he took too much
abuse from Tyson. Spinks wasn't in the best shape for a
fight, really. His knees were shot and crumbling, and his
flesh had a jiggle to it, a tremor of middle age, although he

was just thirty-one. He had never been a true heavyweight, but rather a cruiserweight who put on the extra pounds through diet and exercise. Little wonder, then, that Spinks seemed shy and nervous in public, and uncomfortable in interviews. He relied on his manager, mouthpiece, and closest ally, Butch Lewis, to do his yelling for him, and Lewis performed the task with a vengeance, lunging for the microphones with the fervent, joyous energy of a lounge act on the loose. The machinery of hype was turning, after all, and Butch was a cog in the machine.

The hype machine always showcased the money numbers first, as it did in a press kit embossed with the Trump Plaza crest—a red oval festooned with gold leaves and a beefeater crown. Mike Tyson was grossing twenty million dollars for the fight, I learned from the kit, while Spinks would gross about thirteen million. In addition, Tyson had picked up a million more for some Diet Pepsi commercials, and he was also in the middle of an eight-fight contract with HBO, which gave the network the right to broadcast his bouts, live or on tape, for about twenty-six million dollars. (The contract was null and void if Tyson ever lost.) HBO is a subsidiary of Time, Inc., so surely it wasn't a coincidence that Tyson turned up on the covers of *Time*, *Life*, *People*, and *Sports Illustrated* just before the match.

But regardless of all the noise and publicity, I couldn't blame the fans for being fascinated by a contest that looked competitive on paper. Michael Spinks, although aging, was no tomato can. In thirty-one pro fights, he'd never lost by a decision or a knockout. He had a reputation for trickiness, too—the Spinx Jinx, which he laid on other boxers to mess with their heads. He was cute and smart and quick. Stand up and trade blows with Tyson? No way, José. I figured Spinks would skip and glide and jab, he'd put on his tap shoes and dance, dance, dance until Iron Mike was frustrated and dead on his feet. If the fight went the distance, all twelve rounds, I thought he might even squeak out a victory. Stranger things have happened in boxing, of course, which has always been the strangest sport around.

If Mike Tyson didn't exist, I got the feeling that Seth Abraham of HBO might have invented him, so perfect was Tyson for the medium of TV. Abraham grew up in the shadow of Ebbets Field, in Brooklyn, and he still has a boy's enthusiasm for sports and games, and plays basketball with some friends at least twice a week. Stocky and intense, he has the look of a man who'd sink his teeth into your calf at half-court and not extract them until his team was way ahead. He prides himself on working hard, cares about his family, and loves the pulse of the Big Apple—the pulse of making it and running his own little empire.

When I visited Abraham at his office in midtown Manhattan before the fight, he explained how he had turned boxing into a star attraction for HBO. While reading a newspaper one night, he'd come across an item about the trials of Marvelous Marvin Hagler, a dynamite yet mostly unrecognized middleweight. After almost fifty pro bouts,

Hagler was at the top of the heap, but none of the alphabet organizations (WBC, WBA, IBF, and so on) would give him a title shot. That was partly because he was a lefty—the same as being a Martian, in boxing circles. Lefties confound righties; they go about their business backward, like reflections in a mirror. More to the point, though, Hagler was a "black" black man. He had no style or glitter, no Ali jive, so his appeal to the masses was perceived to be limited, at least by those in control of the purse strings.

An African-American or Hispanic fighter who transcends such barriers is known in television parlance as a crossover—Sugar Ray Leonard, for instance, who is dapper, cool, polished, and handsome enough to make a white audience ignore his color. It's possible for a suburban type to imagine Sugar Ray living next door, maybe even putting on a jokey apron and inviting the neighbors over for a barbecue. On the other hand, who'd want to live next door to Marvin Hagler? He had a shaved head, a baleful stare, and a yeoman's attitude toward his job that came strictly from the loading dock. Marvin had a face off an FBI flier, but Sugar Ray was different, not threatening or abrasive, an actor who stayed in character.

At any rate, Abraham was intrigued by Hagler's plight, and the wheels in his head began to spin. There *had* to be a way to sell a fine boxer like Hagler to the general public, he thought—it was just a matter of the right packaging. What if you shot a buttery three-minute teaser to show that Marvin had a human side, with *him* in a jokey apron grilling burgers for his photogenic kids? What if you hyped the next Hagler bout as though it were a major motion picture, using strobe lights, smoke, and glitter? Then Abraham took it a step further: What if Marvelous Marvin fought in prime time? (Most televised matches are filler material now, slipped into a dull afternoon slot between, say, a dogsled race in Alaska and an ice-skating tournament.) The idea was wonderfully basic, Abraham believed. If a fight aired on Saturday night after copious advance advertising, with the appropriate amount of fanfare, viewers would assume it was a "can't-miss" event and be compelled to tune in.

So Abraham proceeded. He signed Hagler to a three-fight deal with HBO. Hagler demolished Fulgencio Obelmejias in the first bout, and next met Vito Antuofermo, a rock-headed Italian from Bari. The two men had battled before in Las Vegas, and though Marvelous Marvin labored for fifteen rounds like a peasant busting stones with a pickax, all he got for the effort was a controversial draw. That was bad news for him, but not for Abraham, who portrayed the TV rematch as a vital spectacle on a par with the mythic Westerns of Hollywood, where a gunslinger sets out to avenge himself, hoping to win back what he's been robbed of by the law. In front of an ecstatic hometown crowd, in Boston, Hagler won decisively in five, and went on to fulfill his contract by scoring a TKO over Mustafa Hamsho and retaining his world title.

Since those early days, HBO's packaging had become more sophisticated, Abraham told me. The network had added cameras and close-ups—sweat dribbling down a fighter's chest, for example, or blood trickling from a cut above an eye. Knockouts were shown from various angles and in slow motion, so that the boxers stumbled around in an oddly balletic way, like stoned Baryshnikovs. Some trainers agreed to wear mikes, and when they exhorted their charges between rounds, the fans could eavesdrop on the lies. "It's your last chance, kid," a trainer might say, unabashed to be recyling a chestnut. "Only a KO can save you now." HBO hired its own judge, too, who sat at ringside and judged the official judges, and its announcers were dazzling in their tuxedos, as if they were attending a concert at Lincoln Center instead of a donnybrook where two guys were trying to slug each other senseless.

"How have the ratings been?" I asked Abraham.

"Fairly good," he said. "But it's clear that heavyweights draw the best."

That only confirmed an old boxing adage. From time immemorial, the fight game has risen or fallen on the relative strength of its heavyweight division. A giant with a power punch, somebody who can reverse his fate with a single blow, is able to carry all the other divisions on his shoulders. A heavyweight champ should be both noble and indestructible, designed by the Pentagon and prepared to defend the United States of America against its enemies, as Rocky Balboa did in the movies. The record books showed clearly that boxing had hit its last peak during the tenure of Muhammad Ali. Since then, Larry Holmes had been the dominant heavyweight, but Holmes was chubby, bland, and lacked what Ingemar Johansson once called "the hammer of Odin"—that all-important, vaguely nuclear power punch.

So HBO was more than ready for someone like Mike Tyson to come along, according to Abraham. Iron Mike was volatile and exciting, and his story was rich in the pap and pathos celebrated on TV: how he'd been rescued from a life of crime by wily old Cus D'Amato, who had guided Floyd Patterson, another poor black youth, to a crown; how D'Amato had moved Tyson up to the Catskills, into a creaky Victorian mansion where Cus, a sort of Fagin, lived in Dickensian splendor with his sister-in-law and a half dozen boxers in training; how he'd tried to teach Tyson discipline and the sport's history; and how he'd brought in Jimmy Jacobs, a man known for his probity, to serve as Tyson's manager. It was Jacobs who bestowed a congratulatory kiss on Iron Mike's brow whenever he got a knockout.

Here was a story that was perfect for the masses, featuring a heroic central figure who did have nuclear capability. Still, despite all the pluses, when Abraham signed up Tyson, he crossed his fingers and hoped for the best. Boxing, he'd learned, was like no other business. In negotiations, the rule of thumb was to screw the other party before they screwed you; a deal was only solid until a better deal was offered. For instance, Butch Lewis had done so much sly maneuvering lately that HBO was forced to sue him, which meant that Butch, by the legal standards of boxing, was obligated to sue HBO in return.

"I've become an expert on litigation," Abraham said, his eyes twinkling brightly. He told me that he no longer believed a match was really big unless at least two lawsuits were pending. For fun, he toted up the suits that Tyson-Spinks might generate and arrived at an amazing number—eight. Holy cow! The fight, Abraham said, must be a monster.

On the night before the main event, I sat in my hotel room wondering about Mike Tyson's state of mind. He, too, had legal problems, along with emotional problems, and he wasn't handling them very well. As an innocent young fighter, he had depended on Cus D'Amato to supervise his affairs and lend him moral support, but Cus had died and so had Jimmy Jacobs, leaving him without a mentor. When Tyson talked about D'Amato, he did so in mystical terms, as if Cus were a magus, and he saw his transformation from a gutter punk to a famous and wealthy boxer as a miracle of the highest order. Without Cus and Jimmy in his corner, he felt less grounded and sure of himself, in need of someone to guide him, all alone.

More important, Tyson was sunk in domestic woe. He had recently married Robin Givens, a stunning young actress, pursuing her through the nightclubs of Los Angeles like a hunter chasing a trophy. "I suaved her," he jokingly said, when reporters asked him how he'd ever managed to win her hand. In her presence, he seemed to glow and even double in size. It was doubtful that Tyson, even in his most elaborate fantasies, could have imagined himself with such a refined woman. A graduate of Sarah Lawrence, Givens was petite and elegant. She had poise and social grace, and could walk into a crowded restaurant and make the maître d' snap to attention—a feat Tyson could only accomplish with a blow. That he loved her madly was never at issue. She led him around by the nose.

But at the same time, the marriage frustrated Iron Mike. He hated to watch his affairs dragged through the muck of the tabloids. The first accusation to be printed was always that Givens wanted his money; the second was that she needed the publicity. When she became pregnant, the rumor was that she meant to trap him, and when she claimed to miscarry, there were people who believed she'd never been pregnant at all. Then a sister of Givens confided to a reporter that Tyson had beaten Robin, and that she was afraid of him. Meanwhile, another report had Tyson cheating on her with other women, while he was also—supposedly—spending a million bucks a month on jewels and trinkets for his wife.

What could he do about such attacks? Not much, in the end. Tyson had a lot on his plate, I thought. In certain ways, he *was* immature. He argued with his wife, made dumb mistakes, and did things he regretted, just like everybody else on earth. He was grappling with his nature—growing, changing, and striving to be his own person—and it offended him that the world was stomping on his heart. Then, too, Don King had snuck into his life as a kind of unofficial adviser, and had started working on him, telling him he deserved a better shake for his boxing skills. King promised the moon, of course, yet his empire was built on the fact that he sometimes delivered the moon. And with a black fighter, King didn't have to empathize, summarize, sympathize, or editorialize, as he might have put it himself—he had the advantage of *being* black.

So as the fight approached, I assumed that Tyson must be stretched pretty tight. It was a difficult moment for him, a moment when his mind might wander, drifting away from its familiar grooves. For one thing, he wasn't an innocent anymore. A punch to the stomach might not hurt him, but life itself was turning painful. He'd had some humbling experiences in recent months. Tyson couldn't tolerate it when people insulted his wife, and he had wept over his inability to prevent it, wishing he could deal out some retribution in the only way he knew how, with his fists. Boxing had once been a pure joy to him, a means to escape from ghetto oblivion and a future in prison, but the sport was on the verge of being spoiled for him now. He knew too much, and also much too little.

The Atlantic City Convention Center is on the boardwalk, right next to Trump Plaza, so, out of curiosity, I walked over to watch the advance preparations on the afternoon of the fight. A crew of carpenters was pounding nails when I arrived, rearranging boards to expand the seating capacity to twenty-two thousand. A seat at ringside would cost a plunger fifteen hundred dollars; a roost in the highest balcony, up there with the pigeons, ran a cool hundred. From the rafters, the ring looked no more substantial than a scrap of paper somebody had dropped; the boxers would be no bigger than specks of ink. The hall itself was huge and dimly lit—an eerie, resonant space that could have been a leftover set from *The Manchurian Candidate*.

Because the bout was being carried live in about thirty countries, including Paraguay, Gabon, and the Cayman Islands, there were a few foreign reporters getting ready to file dispatches. Two Japanese guys in black cardigans practiced golf swings with invisible clubs, while a miniature sportscaster from England, his socks not quite touching his trouser cuffs, paced up and down an aisle and rehearsed his lines. "In less than an hour," he said, speaking into a rolled-up program, "the most eagerly awaited sporting event in history will take place in this lovely old seaside arena, where the queens of American beauty have always been crowned."

Around four o'clock, while the HBO technicians were doing a sound check, Donald Trump breezed into the hall. Probably he'd been drawn to the spot by a magnetic force flowing from the eleven TV cameras, sucked unavoidably into the limelight. The strange thing was that he didn't appear to be the least bit comfortable. His bearing was stiff and military, as if he were operating under orders from a mysterious government. In fact, a major parlor game among the writers covering the fight was trying to detect Trump's fatal flaw. Vanity? Insecurity? Kinky sex? It wouldn't have surprised anybody to hear that he had a dark secret.

With an aide, Trump toured the floor. He chatted with the technicians, shook a hand here, a hand there—he had the common touch, and I could imagine him in politics someday. Striding to a ringside arena labelled, for some ungodly reason, the VIP Corral, he sat in a folding chair and craned his neck this way and that, as if searching for a clear line of sight. He couldn't find it.

"Frank won't be able to see," he complained to the aide.

The seat, as it happened, was reserved for Frank Sinatra, the Chairman of the Board and the most powerful person in any casino town. Trump was concerned because the ring was too high off the ground. Even if Sinatra tilted his head back, he'd miss part of the action, so Trump summoned Ross Greenburg, HBO's executive producer, and invited him to try out the seat for himself. Greenburg agreed that the line of sight was bad, but he also argued, quite tactfully, that this was often the case at fights. Still, Trump held firm. He couldn't take a chance on Sinatra leaving the convention center in a pissed-off mood after only a round or two.

"Lower the ring, Ross," he ordered.

The blood drained from Greenburg's face. *Lower the ring, Ross:* Here was the mythic Donald Trump in action, the Trump of forceful land grabs and mega-deals. His philosophy was simple and direct—do the job right or don't do it at all. Damn the expense, the eleven cameras that the union guys would have to reposition—hey, what did the union guys care, they were on triple time! In seconds, they went to work with their wrenches and screwdrivers and took everything apart. Down came the ropes, down came the stanchions. Thirty minutes later, the ring was back together again and lower by a foot.

The Convention Center was rocking on fight night, and also star-studded. On my way in, I passed Billy Crystal and Gregory Hines, and compared notes with Norman Mailer. The live gate had exceeded twelve million dollars, the largest take ever for a boxing match, while the drop at Trump's casino would increase by almost twenty million. Up in the balcony, I wandered for a time among a dense concentration of hardcore fans, tough lads from Trenton and South Philly who were belting back the brewskies and could list all the heavyweight champs since John L. Sullivan, the Boston Strong Boy. The fans at ringside were not so versed in the fine points, though. In the front row were some puzzled high rollers who'd been comped in by their hotels, along with some VIPs who couldn't tell a right cross from a double cross.

That accounted for the strangely subdued atmosphere in the Corral, I figured. I'd felt more excitement over at Trump Plaza, where everybody in the ticketless mob wanted a piece of history—a souvenir Tyson-Spinks T-shirt, a logo baseball cap, or a blurry snapshot of an actor emerging from a stretch limo. I saw teenage girls from the projects dressed up and wobbling around on spike heels, hoping to meet someone important—not Mike Tyson, of course, but maybe somebody who worked for him, or who knew somebody who worked for him. They shared the ancient dream of being discovered and swept up from their ordinary lives to a swanky prefight party such as Donald Trump's, where the guests drank Dom Pérignon from elegant stemware and signed their names in a guestbook marked "Celebrities."

The fighters had no sense of the pandemonium on the boardwalk, naturally. They were isolated in drab backstage dressing rooms with members of their respective posses. For Tyson, that meant his trainer Kevin Rooney and a few close friends. Iron Mike's job now was to get his head together and keep it together, so instead of dwelling on his problems he shadowboxed to loud rap music blaring from a radio and recalled the teachings of Cus D'Amato, remembering that he was a hero and not afraid to die. All great fighters try to believe this, but they don't believe it forever. The body isn't invincible; it always breaks down. But Tyson was still young and strong and the more he danced, the better he felt. All the hype would evaporate once he was in the ring, and he would know his true purpose again.

While Tyson was gathering his energies, Butch Lewis staged a scene on behalf of Michael Spinks. Lewis had heard that one of Tyson's gloves was slightly irregular—a tiny piece of tape hung loose—so Lewis lodged a formal protest with the officials. Was he hoping to annoy Tyson and upset his balance by forcing him to wait for the bout to begin? Or could it be that Spinks was so petrified he'd become sick to his stomach and needed more time in the dressing room? No matter: Tyson refused the bait and controlled his anger, throwing two wicked punches into a wall, *bang-bang*, and grinning at Butch as if to say, "Welcome to the House of Pain, Butchie boy."

There is a special look of fear a boxer wears when he knows he's going to lose, and Michael Spinks had it when he climbed through the ropes. His eyes were shifty, glazed over with a peculiar and suspect defiance. His knees were bandaged, his breath came hard, and his head was hanging. He was sweating buckets. I thought he might bolt at any second, dash up an aisle, and run all the way home to Delaware, where he could triple-lock the front door and alert the pit bulls to impending danger. Surely the only thing binding him to Atlantic City was the prospect of collecting the thirteen million dollars he'd earn just for showing up. His anxiety level seemed to rise considerably when Tyson joined him under the lights, wearing black trunks and black shoes and looking every inch a nightmare.

The ring announcer, eager for his moment of fame, launched into a ceaseless tide of introductions. One VIP after another took a bow—old men, bald men, battered fighters, lovely women, but no Frank Sinatra. His seat remained conspicuously empty, Trump's effort be damned. The crowd offered tepid applause, except to Robin Givens and George Steinbrenner, who both got booed; whereas the much-loved Muhammad Ali was awarded a thunderous standing ovation. Everyone respected Ali and was also saddened by him. He had fought with immense daring, he had charm and wit, but he had fought for too long. Now he moved slowly and haltingly, and his quicksilver mind was cloudy. When he visited the challenger's corner, Spinks might well have seen him as an object lesson—a reminder to avoid undue punishment.

After shaking Ali's hand, Spinks knelt in prayer while Tyson—up on his toes, bouncing with barely concealed delight—accepted a hug from Rooney. The bell rang, and he skipped merrily forward, looking not wild or brutal but determined and methodical. He was in no hurry. He planned to take his time, to relax and enjoy himself. That was exactly what Spinks expected from him—to march straight ahead into the fray. During two months of training, in fact, Spinks had been drilled in the art of being a moving target. He was supposed to be slippery, backpedalling and sidestepping as he threw jabs from odd angles, but he ignored or forgot his game plan. Instead of being fluid, he stayed fixed, his feet firmly planted as he, too, marched straight ahead. It was the worst thing he could have done, and soon enough he was paying for it.

Spinks never landed a decent punch. Hampered by his bum knees, he looked unsteady on his feet, and Tyson hit him with several solid shots right off the bat that rattled his composure, tossing in a left elbow to the chin for good measure—a mugger's trick off the mean streets. "Cut it out, Mike," the ref warned, but Tyson was already moving forward again. He pushed Spinks to the ropes and nailed him with a hard left to the jaw, following it with a huge right hook to the chest. The force of the blow was immense, and

Spinks, a boxer who'd never lost as a pro, dropped to one knee, just as he'd done when he was praying.

Spinks would use the opportunity to recuperate, I thought. As a veteran boxer, he'd know enough to cool out, take a long count, and spend the rest of the round backing away from Tyson or tying him up in clinches. But he surprised me—no, he shocked me, really. Again he defied the logic of the situation and did the worst thing he *could* do, jumping up at the count of three and posing flat-footed before his opponent, as if to ask for more of the same. He staggered toward Tyson and led with an amateurish right that left him wide open, and Iron Mike didn't let the chance go by. In a brisk arc, he brought up his own right hand and caught Spinks flush on the side of the head, cutting his legs out from under him and toppling him once more.

There was a loud thump when Spinks fell to the canvas. His shoulders hit it first and then his head hit it, rebounding twice. His eyes were more terrified than squirrelly. I wondered what he was thinking as he lay there stretched out before some twenty-two thousand people. Maybe nothing—a downed fighter often floats along in a semiconscious state. But maybe Spinks was remembering that he wasn't obliged to carry on. He had played his role in the Tyson melodrama, proving again that Tyson was a superhuman puncher. Why risk another blow? It seemed to me that Spinks liked it on the floor, even that he'd willed his own KO and was glad that it had occurred in a hurry. As the clock ticked and the ref counted, he made no honest attempt to get up.

From the bell to the knockout, only ninety-one seconds had elapsed. Ninety-one seconds—the time it takes to brush your teeth! There was a lot of grumbling in the ring-side seats, where the fans were tearing up their ticket stubs and kissing their fifteen hundred bucks goodbye. A man in the row in front of me was late in returning from the rest room and had missed the entire match! It didn't help, either, that Spinks, counted out, was now upright again, smiling sheepishly and being embraced by his cornermen. But for what? That was the question asked throughout the arena. If Spinks hadn't technically thrown the fight, he'd done precious little to make it competitive and obviously didn't deserve the huge check he would be depositing in Delaware.

Most prizefights have an unanticipated wrinkle at the end, a subtle twist of fate, and so it was in Atlantic City when Michael Spinks, the devious loser, walked away looking like a winner. He hadn't stayed on his feet long enough for Tyson to do him any harm, and the money in his back pocket would let him retire in splendor and buy all the fancy clothes he wanted. But Mike Tyson wasn't so fortunate. When he raised his arms in triumph, I saw a look flash across his face that made me concerned about his future. It was a flicker of disappointment, even of confusion, as if for years he'd been hiking up a mountain, only to find on reaching the peak that it afforded him no view, no sunshine.

Why had he bothered to climb it? Tyson lived to box, but he had defeated every contender, and there was no serious opponent on the horizon. So what would his new life at the top be like, where were its passion and its promise? Instead of hanging around a gym and trading quips with D'Amato and Jacobs, he'd be trapped in meetings with attorneys and accountants. He would spend his days idly, maybe shopping for luxury cars or thirty-room houses, and try to be a decent husband to a woman he scarcely understood. His finer emotions would have to be held more tightly in check than ever, because he was the baddest dude on the block now and open to any challenge—the undisputed heavyweight champ of the world, which was meant to be a blessing, not a curse.

7
Feather
River
Country

I AM ALWAYS ON THE lookout for a new stream to fish,
so this autumn I mounted a trip to the North Fork of the
Feather River, where I'd never been before. Its headwaters
are just southeast of Lassen Peak, a dormant volcano, and it
winds downhill for some twenty miles over granite boulders, through Douglas firs and a variety of pines, until it
empties into Lake Almanor. Aquatic birds love the marshes
around the lake, and when they molt their feathers drift
into the stream in huge numbers, creating a spectacle that
caught the eye of Captain Luis Argüello, a Spanish ex-
plorer, back in 1817, and caused him to come up with the
name *El Río de las Plumas*.

From Lake Almanor, the Feather rolls through some
densely timbered country that hides the rustic settlements
of Seneca and Caribou. It rejoins civilization—a relative
term in the woods—at Belden, a hamlet of trailers and

moss-hung cottages grouped around a general store. Hard as it is to believe, Belden was a prosperous gold-mining center in the eighteen-fifties, and so was nearby Rich Bar. The ore was in the mountains and the placers of the streambed, and there was a ton of it. Four lucky miners from Georgia once hauled out fifty thousand dollars' worth of gold from Rich Bar in a single afternoon.

We're fortunate to have an account of the area in its heyday, thanks to Dame Shirley Clappe, a transcendentalist sympathizer from New England. She moved out west with her husband, the frail Dr. Fayette Clappe, and captured the rowdy spirit of the mining camps in her letters home. The Clappes had a momentous journey from San Francisco to Rich Bar, according to one letter. Predictably, Fayette suffered from anxiety and fevers, while Dame Shirley fell off her mule. Her mood did improve, though, when she glimpsed the North Fork from the summit of a hill. She thought it resembled "half a dozen blue-bosomed lagoons, glittering and gleaming and sparkling in the sunlight as if each tiny wavelet were formed of rifted diamonds."

The Feather at Rich Bar is not so stunning anymore, but the stretch below the suspension bridge at Belden, where Yellow Creek pours in, is still impressive. Here the river is big and sweeping, dark green, awash with foam. It flows with such power that it suggests a force of nature just barely held in check. The soaring walls of a canyon pinch it in, and when a freight train chugs by on a track along a canyon wall, you can hear the locomotive working on all cylinders. The past seems not so far away for a moment, but this spot marks the end of the Feather's glory. Hydro dams clog its lower reaches, and it loses its thrust and grows sluggish and tired as it runs through such odd little communities as Pulga and Jarbo Gap.

I traveled through this territory on my drive into the Sierra Nevada and up to Chester, a lumber and cattle town that's situated at an elevation of some forty-five hundred feet. Chester is home to about two thousand people. The September evening was fine and warm, but the maple trees on the main drag were already turning color. I stopped at a pharmacy to buy a tube of toothpaste and also picked up the current issue of *Gold Prospector,* a magazine for the amateur gold hounds who use pans, sluices, and dredges to ply such rivers as the Feather for flakes and nuggets.

I had hoped to rent a cabin in Chester, but I couldn't find one and booked a motel instead. In the motel restaurant—a weird room with a vaguely Polynesian decor that included tiki heads—steak and prime rib were served in triumphant American portions. Full to the brim, I nursed a bourbon at the bar after dinner and made the mistake of asking the bartender how the fishing had been lately. The question had been put to him before. He grunted and said there were *always* fish in Hamilton Branch and High Bridge, at Butt Creek and Butt Lake, downriver in Caribou and even right in Chester. In fact, the North Fork was many different streams, and they all held *plenty* of trout—here he grunted again—for anglers skilled enough to catch them.

The first place I fished was Yellow Creek. I was heading for Caribou, where the fly-fishing was supposed to be good, but I missed the turnoff and wound up parked at a rest area across from the Belden general store. The creek was nearby, tumbling out of a forest of mixed conifers. A trail ran alongside it, so I put on my waders and hiked in for half a mile. Steller's jays, with their fierce crested heads and argumentative squawking, sailed about, settling on the limbs of pines and knocking down pinecones. Gray squirrels were also bustling around and acting like the squirrels in storybooks, gorging on acorns and other nuts in anticipation of winter.

There were lots of big rocks in Yellow Creek. Its flow was not smooth; rather, it was broken up into little pockets. One angling writer, Art Lee, has compared pocket water to an apartment complex for trout. The fish can live fin by tail in spaces as small as three hundred and twenty-four square inches—a foot and a half by a foot and a half—if the spaces are from eight to twelve inches deep. The main problem in fishing such water is that the wading can be difficult. The rocks underfoot are slippery, and the current is usually strong. But pocket water offers significant advantages, too.

Insects bounce by the pockets very quickly, so trout can't waste much time on inspection. In slack water, they examine bugs at their leisure, and they're less likely to mistake an artificial fly for a natural.

From my fly box I chose a medium-sized Humpy. It's a bushy brown dry fly that rides high on the water and can take a good deal of buffeting without losing its shape. Humpies are not necessarily meant to imitate any particular insect that might be hatching. Instead, they're intended to represent a curious but inviting morsel of food to a trout; it's like drifting a filet mignon before creatures who've been eating hamburgers and are ready for a change.

On my first few casts, I raised some fish, but I failed to catch them. They nipped at the fly and disappeared before I could set the hook. I waded on for another ten yards, but I got no more rises, so I stopped in some slanting shade and switched the spool on my reel. The new spool had a sinking rather than a floating line, and I used it to fish a caddis nymph—a fly that duplicates a caddis larva. Almost immediately, I caught and released a nine-inch rainbow trout. I fished for an hour longer, until the sun was almost directly overhead and the creek was translucent. When I climbed up the bank to the trail, I stepped into a cloud of ladybugs. There must have been a million of them. The sky was dotted with orange-red bodies.

That afternoon, when the sun was lower in the sky and there were shadows on the water, I backtracked to Caribou and found the right turnoff—a bumpy macadam road that took me past a deserted trailer park and into mostly wild country. From the road, the river looked deceptively shallow. If you'd never been fishing, you probably would have ignored it, on the assumption that it was fishless, but you would have been wrong. This was pocket water again, and the trout were in their apartments.

The foothills by the stream were tangled with chaparral—greasewood, toyon, chamiso. Dame Shirley hated this stuff. She thought the knotted shrubbery stood like "vegetable skeletons along the dreary waste." Chaparral was "a plantation of antlers," and no fun to scramble through. But I parked the car anyway, and scuttled downhill into a thicket of blackberries. Next to the thicket, there were some manzanita bushes, small and smooth, with twisted reddish limbs. Manzanitas put out a fruiting cluster that looks like a little apple—which is what *manzanita* means in Spanish.

I put the spool with the floating line back on my reel and tied on a fresh Humpy. Because the water level was low, the wading was easy. I fished around a bend and spooked a water ouzel from its perch on a boulder. The ouzel, or dipper, is truly an amazing bird. It's not much bigger than a wren and built the same way, with its tail upturned at an angle. This bird walks on the bottom of streams to get its food. Never mind the rushing turbulence. Ouzels just saunter along, digging into the streambed with their claws and drawing a nictitating membrane over their eyes like a pair of goggles.

I cast into the pocket behind the ouzel's boulder and watched a trout rise and take my fly. It was another rainbow, maybe twelve inches long, but quite fat through the middle—fat enough to make a meal. Trout stay fresher if you clean them right away, so I killed this one and gutted it, and continued my casting. There was a breeze now, and it scattered leaves from the blackberry bushes onto the water, where they made soft ripples and dimples, like feeding fish.

In Rich Bar during the Gold Rush, the only two-story building in town was the Hotel Empire. Dame Shirley was not fond of it. She objected to the scarlet calico of the barroom ("that eternal crimson calico, which flushes the whole social life of the 'Golden State' with its everlasting red") and to the architecture of the place ("such a piece of carpentering as a child two years old, gifted with the strength of a man, would produce, if it wanted to play at making grown-up houses"). I had a similar opinion of my motel, so on the return trip to Chester I scouted the shoreline of Lake Almanor for resorts and discovered Plumas Pines. It had a store, a marina, and several compact, powder-blue cabins. The one I rented was set back from the road, under some fir trees.

I carried my groceries inside and stacked cans and boxes on shelves. Grape-Nuts here, cornmeal there. The fridge wasn't on, so I plugged it in and filled it with beer and soft drinks. I stored the cheese in the proper compartment, and the meat where it was supposed to go. The cabin had a porch with a view of the lake, and I put my notebooks out there, and also the books and magazines I'd brought along.

Had I ever visited such painstaking attention on my own home? Not likely, friends. But this was a cabin by a lake, in the country—a place out of time, with its own set of demands. I found a cast-iron skillet, swept out the bug wings with my sleeve, and slapped in a pat of butter. Then I washed the trout and rubbed it with garlic and salt and pepper. I poured some milk into a saucer, bathed the fish in it, and rolled it in cornmeal. I fried it with some sliced onion and ate it on the porch, while I read a mystery novel. Then I went to sleep.

The next day, I fished at Caribou again and caught some more small trout, including one brown. It occurred to me that I might be neglecting water that held bigger fish, so in the morning I went to Chester to consult with the locals. There are three tackle shops in town, and the first one I came to was Bob's Bait & Bull. Inside, Bob was behind the counter listening to some bull from two young ladies who had been out shooting pool the night before and claimed to have whipped everybody they'd played. The conversation didn't faze me, because if you own a rural business you need people to sling the bull with—especially when summer's almost over and the tourists have gone home.

Bob was a brawny, bearded guy who wore a baseball cap and a down vest. Virtually every Northern California mountain male of a certain age and outdoorsy temperament wears a baseball cap and a down vest. The Levi's go without saying.

"Good morning!" he bellowed, using all the lung power available to him. "Can I help you?" I selected some token Humpies from a display box and asked Bob—just as I'd asked the motel bartender and everybody else I'd met—if he'd heard anything about the fishing. Well, Bob had. Without hesitation, he recommended Butt Lake, in Plumas National Forest, not far from my cabin. Out at Butt, minnows were dying off and floating to the surface of the lake, in a channel directly below a powerhouse. Anglers were catching very large rainbows on minnowlike spinning lures and night crawlers. The trout went seven, eight, even ten pounds, Bob said, raising his right hand as if to take an oath.

The only thing that bothered me about his report was that I didn't want to fish with hardware or bait—I wanted to stick with flies. Bob shrugged at my stubborness and showed me a fly that imitated a minnow. It had a white head and a silvery foil body dotted with black spots. I bought several of them and also some Almanor Specials— nymphs that Bob touted for fishing the mouth of the North Fork, where it joined Lake Almanor, in Chester. "There's some good big browns in there!" he bellowed again. "Just walk on in from East Fourth Street."

I took his advice and followed East Fourth until it stopped, abruptly, at the river. Beyond the river was pasture full of whiteface and Angus cattle. I started down a well-worn path through some aspen trees. There was a serenity to the landscape, a harmonious blending of yellows, golds, rusts, and reds. Autumn is an opportune time to fish for brown trout, really. They begin spawning in October, so they're likely to be on the move. Ordinarily, browns are wary feeders that stick close to home. They are much more difficult to fool than rainbow or brook trout. Some years ago, in an experiment on the Deschutes River in Oregon, browns and rainbows were stocked in equal numbers. Four rainbows were caught for every brown. In a similar experiment in Maine, the ratio was five to one.

It took me about ten minutes to reach the river mouth. A slight haze of vapors rose from Lake Almanor. In some marshes, I saw a flock of Canada geese—ungainly birds, terribly awkward on land, but Thoreau loved them when they formed a harrow and flew over his cottage. "Man pygmifies himself at the sight of these inhabitants of the air," he wrote in his journal. The geese in the marshes didn't fly off when I approached, but they honked like angry motorists and scared a bunch of frogs, who leaped into some mud on the shoreline, burying their heads in it. Whenever frogs perform their panicky jumping act, they make a little screeching noise that sounds like "Eeek!" You have to wonder what sort of fantasy they were involved in while they were sunbathing. Nature distracts all its creatures? Induces meditative spells even in cold-blooded brains?

The North Fork ran smoothly here, without any pockets. I waded into the river and cast upstream, so that the Almanor Special would sink and nudge along the bottom. That's where the browns would be, hiding from the sunshine. The trick in fishing nymphs is to know when you've had a bite. Since a dry fly is fished on top, you can see trout rising up to grab it, and you react accordingly. But nymph action takes place in the invisible depths of a river. You have to imagine what's going on down there, using the few clues that are transmitted to you via your line.

The best nymph anglers are said to be able to set their hooks by intuition, anticipating a fish's bite. They respond to messages that are lost on the rest of us. I got several taps that I thought might be trout, but when I set my hook nothing was there. I caught one rainbow at last, but it was another small one, so I quit fishing around noon and went to the Kopper Kettle for a late breakfast of eggs, home fries, and skull-busting coffee.

Dusk at Butt Lake. From a hillside parking lot, I could see bits of silver floating on the surface of some frothy water that was pouring out of a powerhouse. The water flowed through a concrete channel—it was like a spillway—that fed into the lake proper, where everything was still.

The silver bits were dead minnows. Occasionally, there was a swirl in the midst of them, and a giant trout would appear, flashing a huge dorsal fin. About forty anglers were crowded in on one side of the channel, standing on a jetty and casting at the swirls with minnowlike lures and hooks draped with night crawlers. They were flailing around with an energy that can only be born of monstrous desires.

I felt the way poor Dr. Clappe must have felt when he arrived at Rich Bar to hang out his shingle and found that twenty-nine doctors had preceded him. I took up a position between two anglers and tried casting my fly, but I couldn't get it out far enough, and the channel was much too deep to wade. I had to stand there, handcuffed, and watch as a man farther down the line hooked a trout and brought it cautiously to shore. It was a rainbow, and it weighed a good seven pounds. The man had not prevailed by skill or brain-power—he had been using a gob of worms.

On the other side of the jetty, Butt Creek flowed through a ravine. Nobody was fishing it, but I thought I'd give it a shot—maybe I'd be rewarded for my independence. I used everything from nymphs to Humpies, though, and never raised a fish. There was a sliver of moon above the firs when I got back to my car. Below me, in the channel, anglers were carrying on with their casting, night fishing being legal at the lake.

As I was stripping off my waders, a retired fellow from Sacramento came over for a talk. He was one of those perfectly preserved specimens who pride themselves on never having surrendered to an excessive moment in all their lives. He told me he'd fished the creek that afternoon and had taken three rainbows, all sixteen inches long, using crickets for bait. He said that while he was fishing he'd seen another guy take a brown trout that went twenty-seven inches. The guy had also been using crickets, and he'd needed almost half an hour to land the brown, because he was wearing a revolver on his hip and didn't want to get it wet.

I asked why this guy who caught the trophy brown on goddamn crickets had a revolver with him.

"Snakes," the fellow from Sacramento said.

That evening at Butt Lake had a bad effect on me. No longer was I content with a simple day's fishing. What I wanted was a megatrout. Worse, I wanted it on my own terms. It made no difference to me that the only people catching the big ones were not fooling them but feeding them—I kept fishing flies, dry and wet, lost in a purist's syndrome. Once more, I went to Butt Creek—at dawn, this time—and in weather that was cold enough to put frost on my windshield I cast over pocket after pocket without causing a stir.

After that, in a desperate mood, I began to explore. One morning, I fished some slow-moving water of the North Fork at Virgilia, downriver from a couple of optimists who were panning for gold. The pans looked like pie plates, though thicker. When you're panning, you try to concentrate the heavier materials by washing away successive layers of lighter grit. You sift out gravel and lumps of clay, and you wind up with mostly black sand and maybe traces of platinum, tin, and other minerals. If you're lucky, you find a few gold flakes or particles. These you pick out with a pair of tweezers. Sometimes the odd nugget turns up, and a modern prospector makes a little money.

Did I realize then that I was doing the same thing that the panners were doing? That a big brown trout was only slightly less rare than a gold nugget? I did not. Skunked again, I drove to my cabin and passed the evening reading *Gold Prospector*. The editor called himself Buzzard. The first line of his editorial was "All that glitters isn't gold." There were advertisements for sluices, rock crushers, dredges, and a dry-vac backpack gold concentrator, the E-Z Pikins. A full-color centerfold featured photographs of pans dusted with gold. Woody Caldwell, whose column ("Ask Woody") fields questions from readers, discussed the various precious metals that had been used to build New Jerusalem, as they were described in Revelation 21:18–21: "The city was pure gold, like unto clear glass. . . ."

I slept on Woody's vision.

The next day, I was up at dawn again, madly navigating the back roads of Plumas County. I drove halfway around Lake Almanor and fished the Hamilton Branch of the

Feather, where the terrain was daunting. As soon as I climbed over one rock, there was another one ahead of me. I could have been in the infantry. Between rocks there were ugly clumps of grass. There were many overhanging branches waiting to snag my line and foul a cast. I caught nothing on the Hamilton Branch, but it was not the dumbest point of my trip. That came later at High Bridge, outside Chester, the same afternoon. There I covered a mile of pockets—perfect pockets!—in three hours, but all I got was a pair of eight-inch hatchery rainbows.

While I was stretched out on the bank of the river, recovering from my travail, a cricket crawled over my hand. It set off a chain reaction in my head that went something like this: cricket; fellow from Sacramento; three big trout. Without any further thinking, I tapped the cricket with a stone. He quit moving. In my vest I had some hooks, and I took one out and tied it to my leader. Then I put the cricket on the hook and let my line drift into the Feather. No trout rose to the bait. The hook just drifted along, apparently as unappetizing as a leaf or a twig.

I waited about thirty minutes before I reeled in my line. I hoped that the cricket had fallen off, but it was still there, waterlogged and coming apart. The sight of it made me feel cruel and unenlightened. I didn't like to admit that I was capable of such random mayhem. In the city, it's easy to explain those acts away. The cabbie was a jerk. The child deserved to be spanked. The boss does it, too. But solitary expanses of country deprive you of your excuses. To be alone in nature is to be responsible in some ultimate sense.

The only thing that saved this day was the sunset. Is it possible to write about sunsets anymore? Probably not, although it may be necessary. Suffice it to say that this one was brilliant and radiant, with striking aftereffects—streaks of red, then a dull-lavender glow above the pines.

Buoyed up on beauty, I paid a visit to Eidhammer's Chester Saloon and Dining Emporium, where a party was going on. It was Bruce Eidhammer's eighth anniversary as owner, and the drinks were on the house. In the general uproar, I carried on a loud conversation with an old rancher in overalls. He kept circling around a Yamaha electric piano that an entertainer was supposed to play later in the evening. The rancher couldn't figure out how the hell it worked. When the bartender asked him if he needed another beer, he said, "I don't need it, but I'm a-gonna have it."

I told him I'd been enjoying myself in Chester, even though the fishing was slow. He tapped me on the shoulder and said sure, he knew all about it, he'd lived in town for over thirty years. "Fish or no fish, people here will help you out," he assured me. "And that's the truth of it."

Greenville is an old quartz-mining town about twenty-five miles from Chester. I drove there the next morning to take a break from the North Fork and heal my troubled mind. The streets were jammed with kids from Greenville High

School. They had a football game on the weekend, and several jocks in numbered jerseys were cruising around in pickups and shouting about the pain they planned to inflict on their opponents. In Greenville, it was still 1962. It was Frankie Avalon and Annette Funicello, and it was not so bad. The shopkeepers, observing the parade from the sidewalk, were going on about deer season. They talked about nailing bucks on hunting trips to real cowboy country, like Wyoming or Montana.

Although I'd wanted to avoid any fishing, I saw a sign for Round Valley Reservoir, a lake in the mountains above Greenville, and went to have a look at it. The road in was steep and winding. Aspens were blazing in the midst of Douglas firs. Stumps and withered limbs of trees stuck up out of the water—skeletons from the forest that had been drowned when Round Valley was built. There was a considerable growth of moss on the lake, offering a habitat that seemed ideal for largemouth bass. Largemouths thrive in a weedy environment, protected by the abundant cover it provides. In the trunk of the car I had a spinning rod and reel, so I thought I'd do some casting, in case some bass might really be around.

The difference between spinning and fly casting lies mostly with the reel. A spinning reel has a fixed spool. When you cast with it, the weight of the lure uncoils your line and pulls it out. By contrast, a fly is almost weightless. What you actually cast with a fly rod is your line. Fly line is heavy. The earliest types were made of braided horsehair, but now they are usually nylon coated with heat-cured plastic. The line used on spinning reels is called monofilament—a single strand of nylon, much like the leader material you tie to the end of a plastic-coated fly line. Spinning tackle, which originated in Europe, became popular in the United States in the nineteen-forties, and in many respects it represents a technological advance over fly tackle. Yet the best and most discriminating anglers always prefer to fish for trout with flies. This is something of an anomaly in sporting life. You don't find tennis players tossing out their jumbo graphite racquets and replacing them with old-fashioned wood.

I grabbed a Jitterbug from my tackle box. It's a terrific lure, with a plastic body from which treble hooks are suspended. It has a scoop-shaped metal paddle in front of its little white eyes, and the paddle raises a ruckus on the water when the lure is reeled in. Bass mistake it for a frog or some other noisy critter.

After I'd been casting my Jitterbug for a while, I noticed a commotion going on, above some reeds in the water. Dragonflies were swirling around, involved in some sort of mating ritual. There were fifty or sixty of them, and they were in such a frenzy that their wings made a distinct whirring sound. I leaned my rod against a rock and sat on the ground to watch them.

Dragonflies are widespread in temperate regions of the world, and they've been studied rather carefully: an English scientist once studied their activities in a bomb crater in Dorset, in fact. Sight is their most highly developed sense, but they are often fooled by reflections—a pool of oil on a highway, a shimmering automobile top, a shiny black streak on a laboratory bench. When they have doubts about the reality of a pond or a stream, they check their impression of it by touching their abdomens to it. In dragonfly literature, this is known as "behavior directed toward testing the nature of a reflecting surface."

The abdomen of the male dragonfly may be important during courtship. Females are said to be attracted by a show of abdominal color. The desire to copulate is not always reciprocal in dragonflies, though. Sometimes the male has to force the issue. Sometimes the female is initially responsive and then cools down. If that happens, the male strokes the tip of her abdomen with his expanded hind tibiae, or leg joints. He may also draw her abdomen toward his genitalia. All this goes on aloft, while the male carries the female in the tandem position, holding her by the neck. When they're ready to copulate, they shift into the copulation-wheel position, in which the female's genitalia are placed opposite the male's. The time of copulation varies from species to species. Once it's over, the female flies off to deposit the fertilized eggs.

Some of the dragonflies at Round Valley Reservoir were definitely copulating. They didn't appear to take very long— no more than a minute or so. Other dragonflies were engaged in aerial battles over turf. They went at one another with an intent to cause some damage, zooming and diving, like dog-fight pilots over the Coral Sea.

I was struck by how many different things were going on at once in this minute corner of the globe. For the dragonflies, this *was* the globe, of course—some reeds, a lake, hazy air, dusty ground. Shortly after mating, they'd be dead. Maybe they knew about other dragonflies in Malaysia or Africa, but I doubted it. Nature is a single-minded kamikaze when it comes to species propagation. There is a tendency in us human beings to place ourselves above the web of life that supports us, but all it takes is a confrontation with dragonflies to register our similarities even to insects. Frankie Avalon loves Annette Funicello, but Dwayne Hickman's trying to ace him out. The dance goes on and on, whether or not we know we're dancing.

I never did find out if there were any bass in Round Valley Reservoir. My spinning rod stayed propped against the rock, and I sat watching the dragonflies until dark.

On my last day on the North Fork, I returned to Caribou, did some more floating of Humpies over the pockets, and caught seven fish. The biggest, a brown, went thirteen inches—not anything that Bob of Bob's Bait & Bull would want to preserve with his Polaroid, but a nice trout anyhow. I unhooked the brown and sent it on its way. It swam off into a deep pool, where it would lounge around, wilier now, and stuff itself with ants and hoppers and mayflies until it was as stout as a Düsseldorfer with a taste for beer and wurst. Then somebody would probably catch it on a night crawler. Even fish are subject to inflated desires. Oh, this world is mean!

In the morning, I packed up the cabin and took a last walk by the lakeshore. In the shallows, off a wobbly dock, two grebes were dipping their slender necks into the water and chasing minnows. I was going to take the same route home that I'd taken coming up from San Francisco, but at Indian Bar—a fork in the road—I turned left instead of right and followed the river in another direction, toward Quincy, the county seat.

Do you understand that this was all new water? I pulled over, opened the trunk of the car, and got out my fly rod again. The Feather was broad and fast-flowing where I waded into it. About twenty yards ahead of me, I saw a piece of machinery that turned out to be a suction dredge. Somebody was using it as a hydraulic sluice for gold. "Nothing is more shiny or more rewarding to find than those gold nuggets that one pulls out of a gravel bank," Buzzard wrote. *Behavior directed toward testing the nature of a reflecting surface.* Under a low-slung limb of a cottonwood, there was a sudden perturbation of the water, and then a swirling movement, and then a dorsal fin. I started casting.

8
Dreaming

A RACETRACK EXISTS as a world apart, rich in its own mysteries and subject to laws of its own devising. When you walk through the turnstiles at Santa Anita Park, near Pasadena, you could be going back in time to an era of Hollywood glory and entering a grand Art Deco hotel of the thirties. There are curved mirrors and etched glass, imported Mexican tiles and semiformal gardens where punters sit reading the *Racing Form* in a sea of flowering bougainvillea, as if they were waiting for a bellhop to grab their luggage, or a cigarette girl to deliver some smokes. The chance of bumping into a retired movie star in the private turf club is extremely high, as is the opportunity to soak up the last fading essence of Southern California class.

I had come to Santa Anita to have a look at Snow Chief, a Cal-bred colt, who was the current morning-line favorite to win the Kentucky Derby. It was a rainy March afternoon when I arrived, and the distant San Gabriel Mountains had turned a deep and alluring shade of green. Mel Stute, the colt's trainer, was in his grandstand box, where I caught up with him and had some coffee to ward off the chill. In his many years on the backside, Stute has had only one previous Derby candidate, Bold and Rulling, so I had no problem forgiving him when he mentioned Snow Chief in the same breath as John Henry, then the leading money-winner in racing history.

Some trainers appear never to have mucked out a stall, but Stute isn't one of them. He's a hard worker whose sixtieth birthday is fast approaching. Warm and friendly, he has the leathery face of a cowboy and seems full of energy. Around the clubhouse, he wears a tie and jacket, but I was sure he got out of the monkey suit as soon as humanly possible and back into his jeans. His first job in racing was rubbing horses for his older brother, Warren, but that didn't give him any edge as a trainer. Instead, he labored at such minor-league tracks as Golden Gate Fields and Portland Meadows before rising into the majors and making his reputation as a clever handler of claimers, buying and selling cheaper stock with the acumen of a poker shark.

The second race of the day was about to go off, so we quit talking to watch it. Stute had two maiden geldings entered, Bride's Advice and Lord Prevue, and when the gate snapped open, he began moving his arms back and forth in unison, as if he were skiing cross-country. I thought this must be a trick of his for attracting good fortune. Every gambler relies on such gimmicks. One friend of mine refuses to go to the track unless he has on his red socks, the way Alexander Calder, in old age, favored red flannel shirts for effect. My own trick is to never hold on to a losing ticket, for fear it will contaminate my aura and keep me from ever cashing a bet.

Anyhow, Stute was skiing for victory. It didn't help Bride's Advice, who took a misstep and threw his rider, but Lord Prevue was operating under a benign influence and finished first at a generous price of twenty-five to one. That had Stute whooping, and he let an admirer in the next box buy him a drink. His popularity around Santa Anita has never been higher—a Derby-bound colt will do that for a man. Fans came toward him in a steady stream, among them a heavyset guy in baggy trousers with a paper bag under his arm. The bag contained a sketch of Secretariat mounted on cardboard, and he gave it to Stute and stood there waiting to be appreciated.

"Why, thank you!" Stute said, handing it over to a bartender for safekeeping. "I don't know what my wife's going to say about it. She thinks we already have too many pictures of horses."

"A friend of mine did that," the man said proudly, drumming up business. "He's an artist. He used, what do you call it?"

"Charcoal?"

"No, not charcoal. Pencils. Anyway, Mel, if you ever want a drawing of Snow Chief, he'll be glad to do it for you."

Stute had been reunited with his prize colt earlier in the week, when Snow Chief returned from Gulfstream Park after winning the five-hundred-thousand-dollar Florida Derby. It was his most impressive performance to date. Breaking from the twelve hole at the outside of the field, he'd had to use up some of his speed to get to the front, but he had more than enough left over and turned the race into a convincing demonstration of his ability to cover a mile and an eighth. Snow Chief is not supposed to do such things. His breeding is unspectacular. He once raced at a cheap track in Mexico, for example, and he bucked his shins as a two-year-old. He should be an ordinary claiming type, not a potential star, but he continues to learn and grow. One of the raps against Cal-breds is that they don't travel well, but Snow Chief had no trouble in Florida and remained unfazed by the bright lights and popping flashbulbs.

Still, Stute was slow to accept the fact that Snow Chief might be special. The race that truly convinced him was the Del Mar Futurity last summer. Snow Chief came up from Agua Caliente, in Tijuana, where he'd been resting his bucked shins under the care of Wilfrido Martinez, a Mexican trainer, and Stute did not have time to condition the colt for a long race. He just blew him out around the first turn at Del Mar and hoped for the best. Although Snow Chief wound up losing the Futurity by two lengths, he lost it to Tasso, who went on to become the two-year-old champion.

In the fall, at Santa Anita, Snow Chief ran in the Norfolk Handicap and beat Louisiana Slew, a son of Seattle Slew, who'd cost almost three million dollars as a yearling. Despite the fine performance, Alex Solis, Snow Chief's regular jockey, noticed that the colt was holding something back, and suggested that Stute add some blinkers. Snow Chief has worn them in his last four races and has won all four handily, bringing his record to eight victories in twelve starts and suggesting that he is the genuine article, indeed.

The most common knock you hear against Snow Chief is that he has been racing too often. Valuable two-year-olds are usually turned out for a rest during the winter, but Stute has kept the colt in training, running him on an average of once a month. There are those who believe that such hard work ruins young horses, and that Snow Chief has already reached his peak, yet Stute doesn't believe it and plans to stick to his schedule right up to the Kentucky Derby.

The man who bred Snow Chief, Carl Grinstead, stopped by the box later that afternoon, while Stute went off to saddle a horse. Grinstead, a retired electronics engineer, used to have a factory near Santa Anita and bought his first horse, Eventuate, with a couple of friends. Of all the people around Snow Chief, he is the least surprised by the colt's talent. He had expected speed to show, because Snow Chief's dam, Miss Snowflake, had it in abundance. In Grinstead's opinion, the major test for Snow Chief will be whether or not the colt can cover the classic distances. He would like to see that happen if only to prove to the racing establishment that Cal-breds, even cheaper ones, should be granted some respect.

Grinstead has a partner in Snow Chief, Ben Rochelle, who soon joined us in the box. A former vaudeville dancer, Rochelle made his big money in real estate after he quit show biz, but he was more interested in talking about Betty Grable. He informed me that he had played the Strand and the Paramount and worked in pictures with Marion Davies. He thought I might want a photo of him and his dancing partner, so he said to Grinstead, "Carl, you've got some photos of me, haven't you?"

"I haven't got any photos of you," Grinstead replied, sounding amused.

Unperturbed, Rochelle carried on. "I saw where Snow Chief is three to one in Las Vegas to win the Derby."

"You'd be crazy to take those odds, Ben," said Grinstead. "You'll get a better price at Churchill Downs."

Grinstead and Rochelle are both in their seventies and refer to themselves as the Sunshine Boys, after the Neil Simon comedy. They are nothing like the Sunshine Boys, really, except insofar as they enjoy the limelight. When they became partners—Grinstead sold Rochelle half of his entire operation—neither of them suspected that they were closing a deal that included a million-dollar colt. In that sense, they resemble a couple who embarked on an affair and wound up committing marriage. The main thing is that both Grinstead and Rochelle are exceptionally happy to be associated with a famous horse.

"Did I tell you I'm going to be on TV in Mexico, Ben?" Grinstead asked. "I'll be talking about Snow Chief on *Tijuana: Window to the South.*" He said this with a straight face.

Stute had told me that some officials from Garden State Park, in New Jersey, had urged to him run Snow Chief in the Garden State Stakes, which would qualify the colt for a million-dollar bonus. But it would also force him to interrupt his successful training schedule and compete in a race only two weeks before the Derby, so Stute refused. I was curious about Grinstead's reaction.

"I've got a little money set aside," he said, implying that he was above such temptations. "If you win in Kentucky, you go down in history. The Triple Crown races are like the Indianapolis 500 or the World Series."

"People try to buy Snow Chief," Rochelle said smugly.

"They try," his partner agreed. "And we tell them he's not for sale."

I arranged to visit Mel Stute's barn the next morning, and got up at five-thirty. The rain had stopped during the night, and now the weather was cold and clear. From the window of my motel room, I could see the crests of the San Gabriels dusted with fresh snow.

Light was just coming into the sky when I reached Santa Anita, but the backstretch was already bustling. I walked down a muddy lane between barns, dodging riders who were taking their mounts to the training track for a gallop. The barns were wooden and painted a grayish-green. I saw a sleek-feathered rooster with a brilliant-red comb parading in front of several hens on a patch of grass. Goats were hiding in the dark of shed rows. There were grooms whistling as they pitchforked straw from stalls, glad to be out in the fresh air and doing work that brought joy to the muscles. I caught a whiff of coffee and then a whiff of tobacco, and I began to feel alive myself. In fact, I *was* alive and wandering around a racetrack, and at that moment, with oxygen and sunlight flooding every cell of my body, I wouldn't have wanted to be anywhere else on earth.

Stute has Barn 97, in esteemed territory reserved for gentlemen of power. I found him in his rustic, minimalist office, where he keeps a desk, a space heater, and an armchair for visitors. I think somebody had attacked the armchair with a baseball bat. Trainers prefer such quarters, though, because they hate to admit that they're involved in big business. In horse-racing circles these days, you need some basic management skills; intuition and an affection for animals aren't enough anymore. Stute has thirty-two stalls in his barn, the maximum allowed at Santa Anita, and he boards horses elsewhere as well, bringing them over by van when they're supposed to run. He has to spend a lot of time on paperwork, making certain that his owners are billed for feed, veterinary charges, and other costs. It isn't a task he enjoys.

"Well, good morning!" he roared in greeting. "Have you seen the big horse yet?" He calls Snow Chief "the big horse" for obvious reasons. He also calls Snow Chief "the little horse," because he's slightly smaller than average. Both are terms of endearment.

Stute led me down a shed row to a stall that looked no different from any other stall. Show Chief had his head stuck out over the half door, and he was taking in the action around him. He is an alert and lively colt, who nips at his handlers a bit too hard. Almost pure black, he has a white star on his forehead. His conformation is not striking, but he has strong hindquarters and uses them to dig in when he's on a track. He never quits, and mud doesn't bother him at all. Another thing that sets him apart is his intelligence; he is eager to learn and masters his lessons quickly. Sometimes he can be lazy, gliding by on the grease of his talent. If a horse can be said to have a sense of humor, I think Snow Chief may have one.

Stute left me with the colt and his groom, Miguel Hernandez, who is known as Mena. Like everybody around Snow Chief, Mena is riding high. He got into the stall and used a currycomb on Snow Chief, applying the strokes with a firm but gentle touch. He ran a brush through the colt's mane and tail until they looked silky, while he listened to the radio news in Spanish. Mena has a broad Indian face and sparkling eyes. His English is only fair, so we conversed in smiles and one-syllable words. Yes, Mena agreed, this Snow Chief, he is a very nice kind of horse.

When the combing was done, Mena brought out Snow Chief and led him to an open area where there was a hose on the ground. The colt had worked the day before and had wraps on his front legs that needed to be washed off. Another groom held the colt while Mena sprayed his legs and peeled off the tape. "We walk him now," Mena said. From a shed he grabbed a horse blanket, threw it over Snow Chief's back, and cinched it under his belly. He was really grinning now. "Champion!" he said, with enthusiasm. The other groom put his hands to his lips, made loose fists, and pretended to be playing a trumpet. He played the trumpet call you hear before every race, and Snow Chief's ears perked up, as if he were ready for the starting gate.

The groom took the reins from Mena and walked the colt around the shed row, following a circular path. At first, Snow Chief dogged it. He seemed to be having trouble finding a rhythm, but by the third go-round he had himself in gear. The groom was singing softly to him. Who knows what the song was about? Nights in Mexico, a deserted beach, a beautiful woman with a gardenia in her hair. Maybe Snow Chief was listening, or maybe he heard something else—the warbling of finches and the cooing of doves. He went around and around, tossing his head from side to side in a contented way. What a dizzy colt! He was suspended in his own motion, endlessly delighted, full of himself.

Stute showed up after he had finished his paperwork, and he asked me if I wanted to go stand by the rail and watch the horses gallop. It was almost eight o'clock, and the morning had become warm and mild. As we strolled along,

Stute greeted friends and acquaintances, and accepted some good-natured ribbing. The gist of it was that he had finally got lucky. For years, he had been a regular guy, but now he was on the brink of something more significant, and everybody was waiting to see if he would break ranks with the democratic fraternity of the backstretch and turn into a titan of the turf, like D. Wayne Lukas, who had thoroughbreds competing in several states and ran his operation with the cool authority of a corporate C.E.O.

"If I was interested in money, I'd have picked another line of work," Stute whispered, behind a hand. "There are easier ways to be a millionaire."

I wondered if he honestly thought Snow Chief could win the Derby.

"Oh, he's got a real good chance!" He paused and shook his head. "But you just never know for sure. Every horse is a mystery."

There were trainers, jockeys, grooms, and jockeys' agents hanging around the rail in front of the grandstand. The main track was a muddy mess, so the horses were on the training track, which was quite far away. You couldn't watch them properly unless you had a pair of binoculars. Stute did some business with an agent, making arrangements for a mount, and then we bought some coffee and doughnuts at Clockers' Corner.

We sat at a table outside with Warren Stute, whom Mel refers to affectionately as "a tough old bird." Warren is sixty-four, lean and wiry, and he still rode his own horses when they went for a gallop. He had a slash of dried mud clinging to his cheek. Around Mel, he shows all the hard edges of an older brother, proud and jealous by turns.

"I remember back in 1950," Warren told us, reminiscing. "I had a horse called Great Circle, who was third in the Santa Anita Derby. That was a big race even back then. Anyway, his owner wanted to send him to Kentucky and was willing to foot the bill for an express railroad car. Mel was still working for me at the time, and he got all excited. We were going to the Derby! Well, I took him aside and asked him to cool it. 'Hell, Mel,' I said. 'After this, we'll be going to the Derby every year. We've got it made!'"

"So Great Circle ran?" I asked.

Warren laughed. "No, he didn't run, after all. And when I did go to the Derby years later, I went with a fifty-to-one shot, Field Master. He ran like he was fifty-to-one! We tried to get a cab back to the hotel after the race, and there must have been six hundred people lined up outside Churchill Downs."

"I'll be staying at the Galt House down there," Mel said. He doesn't travel much, although he did once take a vacation in New Zealand. While he was there, he bought a horse.

He saw Alex Solis sitting at another table, with his agent. Solis had his riding helmet on, and he was eating a bacon-and-egg sandwich on toast.

"Tell him about Snow Chief," Stute instructed the jockey.

"That colt's very intelligent," Solis said shyly. The egg was sliding on him, about to escape from the bread, but he grabbed after it and made the rescue.

"Alex just bought a house around the corner," the agent offered. "Where is it, Alex? Next door to Eddie Delahoussaye?"

"Near Eddie. Gary Stevens lives near me, too."

I pictured a whole neighborhood of jockeys, with ceramic statues of big people on their lawns.

As we talked further, Solis lost his shyness and talked about himself. A graduate of the Panama Jockey School, he won his first race in Panama City when he was seventeen, and moved to Florida a year later, where he soon developed into a hot property. His transfer to California was relatively recent, but he was already sixth in the standings at Santa Anita and thrilled to be in the presence of such greats as Laffit Pincay and Chris McCarron. He looked on his success as a chocolate sundae and Snow Chief as the cherry on top.

"When you say he's a smart colt, Alex," I wondered, "how do you know it?"

"If we're in a race and I see a hole, I ask him to go through it," he explained. "But he doesn't move right away. Instead, he waits. And the hole, it gets bigger. Then he goes."

"A dumb horse wouldn't do that?"

"No."

The sun was higher in the sky now, and I closed my eyes for a minute and felt the heat seep into my bones. Spring was in the air. When I opened my eyes again, I said, "So Alex, you like this Snow Chief?"

"I don't like him," Solis said, with a smile. "I love him."

2
Only the
Bull Is Safe

If you ask Manuel Correia, a retired butcher from the Azores, how he came to promote bloodless bullfights in his adopted home state of California, he shrugs and smiles. "The bulls obsess me," he'll tell you. "I am an addict. I'm crazy for the bulls." On his ranch in Madera, in the San Joaquin Valley, Correia breeds brave bulls from Mexican stock and spends his idle hours listening to bullfight music and studying bullfight videos. He thinks nothing of driving 400 miles to watch a fight. From his backyard he has a fine view of his own private bullring. The sight gives him immense pleasure. "I owe everything to the bulls," he says.

Correia shares his obsession with many other Portuguese-Americans in the valley, mostly dairy farmers who take part in an annual bullfight season that runs from spring until fall and features corridas at 14 rings. The fights are steeped in nostalgia and tradition, complete with brass bands that play the classic paso dobles marches. Matadors often appear on the same card with rejoneadores, who perform on horseback in the style of the old Iberian nobility. It's no accident that the leading cavalier in the San Joaquin is Joe Correia, Manuel's youngest son, who rides with talent and courage, and who dreams of turning pro someday and performing before huge crowds in Portugal.

The world of bullfighting in California is shadowy and mysterious, half hidden from public view. The fights are usually advertised only in the Portuguese-American media, and some participants want to keep it that way, even though everything is legal and the bulls never shed a drop of blood. But others are proud of the fights as a cultural legacy, and they believe the sport should be promoted more vigorously to attract a larger audience, because only when real money rolls in will the quality of the corridas improve.

Last October there was a corrida in Tulare, not far from Madera, and the Correias didn't want to miss it. The ring was set up in a cavernous building ordinarily used for exhibits of farm machinery. About two thousand fans packed the bleachers, not only leathery old cowpokes but also women and children, just as you'd find in the Azores, where bullfighting is a part of village life. The atmosphere was festive, as at a church bazaar or a county fair.

The bulls were in a corral, swishing their tails to ward off hordes of flies. They came in a variety of colors—black, brown, gray and even chestnut—and weighed about 900 pounds each. They were smaller than Spanish bulls, which routinely top 1,000 pounds. They seemed calm, but that would change the instant the corrida started. The idea was to keep them in the dark until then, so they would be angry and confused in the ring and go on the attack, as the breed had been doing for centuries. Fighting bulls are so intelligent that they are allowed to fight only once. They learn so quickly that they can never be fooled again by the tricks of a torero. "It takes a man twenty years to become a matador," Manuel told me, "but a bull can master a matador in 20 minutes."

The evening began with a paseo—a parade of dignitaries and little beauty queens in tiaras. When the first matador, Paul Pinto of Portugal, was in position, the corral gate snapped open and a bull shot forth as if from the barrel of a gun. No matter how often you've seen this furious rush, it takes your breath away. Bulls can be faster than racehorses over a short stretch. In a herd they feel safe and shy from human beings, but when they're alone and provoked, they'll charge anything that moves, as this bull did. Pinto deflected him with a cape, and the bull came to an abrupt stop and looked puzzled. His great chest heaved, and mucus streamed from his nostrils in gouts.

At such moments bulls appear to be stymied and harmless, but that's a dangerous illusion. They can switch on the power again in a flash. Pinto passed sloppily with his cape and caught a horn in the butt as he scrambled over a wall. Fortunately the sharp tip of the horn had been shaved off, as is the custom in bloodless fights, or he might never have sat down comfortably again. Only his dignity was wounded, though, so he slipped back into action, holding a pair of banderillas in his hands—wooden dowels wrapped in tinsel, with a steel point at the end. He ran at the bull, sidestepped neatly and placed the banderillas in the hump of muscle at the animal's neck. The steel points didn't pierce the bull's hide; instead, they landed in a thick patch of protective Velcro.

Pinto brought out the cape known as a muleta for the fight's last act. It was made of red serge and was smaller than his first cape. He teased the bull into a series of charges, stamping his foot and crying, "Eh, toro, toro!" but the bull was growing tired, and Pinto finally walked away, his back to the horns in defiance. Some cows with clanging bells trotted into the ring to lead the bull back to the pen, accompanied by two cowherds. That's how a fight ends in Portugal. The bull dies at a slaughterhouse, not by a matador's sword in front of the crowd. In the San Joaquin, the bull isn't killed.

The fight was entertaining, and the crowd seemed to enjoy it, but Joe Correia had not been impressed. He thought that the ring was in poor shape, with bad footing that was caused by the slippery, fine sand. Nor did he approve of the lighting—it was too bright, he said, and that distracted the bull. Manuel felt the bull was not aggressive enough, but animals that charge indifferently are not uncommon in the valley. Only one bull in five proves to be a worthy opponent, according to Manuel, partly because the breeding industry in the San Joaquin is so new. Still, he maintained high hopes for the upcoming corrida in Thornton, where Joe would saddle up his horses and have a chance to be a star.

In the U.S. bloodless bullfighting has a curious history. It has cropped up at various times in various places, most notably at the old Astrodome in Houston, where 107,000 spectators took in a trio of fights in 1966. Despite an honest effort to keep the bull from being injured, there is always an outcry from those who find the sport cruel and worry that it represents the first step toward far more brutal contests in the Spanish or Mexican style. On the other hand, bullfight purists can't stand bloodless fights and consider them a mockery. One disgusted aficionado has compared them memorably to "sex without an orgasm." Manuel Correia was unaware of all this controversy when he promoted his first corrida in the San Joaquin and immediately found himself in hot water.

Manuel was born on Terceira, the third largest island in the Azores, to a poor farming family. He left home at nineteen, in 1958, to seek his fortune, stopping first in Brazil and next in California, first in Artesia, then in Mira Loma, where relatives helped set him up as a butcher. He didn't return to Terceira until 1971, when he had enough money for an extended vacation. His trip coincided with the start of bullfighting season. Although Manuel wasn't a huge fan, he went to a fight for fun and loved it. In essence, he had a mystical experience he still can't describe—the birth of a passion, an obsession. He stayed four months and attended 74 bullfights, probably a record even for an Azorean.

When he got back to Mira Loma, life without a bullfight seemed boring, so Manuel acquired some Brahma bulls and tried to teach them to charge but failed. Only bulls bred for the ring would suffice, so he traveled to Mexico and bought nine of them. He put on his first fight, in Visalia, California, on May 10, 1975, counting on his fellow Portuguese-Americans to turn out in force. The event was a great success, and he planned to repeat it, but somebody warned him that bullfighting was illegal in California. "You'd be in jail by now," he was told, "except the mayor here is Portuguese."

Instead of going underground, Manuel took the high road. He appeared before a city and county commission in Riverside County to request a special permit to conduct fights, but he lost when the Humane Society objected. The next day, though, he learned about a provision in the California penal code that allows a bloodless bullfight to take place if it is an expression of a group's cultural or religious heritage. In fact, that was Manuel's goal—to re-create the village scene in Terceira. He got a second hearing, won his permit and dedicated his next corrida to the Holy Spirit.

The corrida didn't go unnoticed. There were protests this time, but the complaining seemed wrongheaded to Manuel, who believes his bulls are treated better than rodeo bulls and far better than the beef cattle that wind up as Big Macs. Besides, Manuel is attached to his bulls for the good luck they've brought him. The land in Madera he bought for them to roam has appreciated and selling part of it made him such a wealthy man that he put down his butcher's cleaver forever.

Now Manuel concentrates on his breeding program and on training horses in the special techniques of el rejoneo. He runs the ranch with Joe, who began performing as a forcado, or bull grabber, when he was fifteen. Teams of forcados are part of the Portuguese tradition and appear only at horseback shows, where they force the bull to a standstill after a cavalier is done with it. Joe was often the lead man of the team, who taunts a bull into charging and then grabs it by the neck while the others pile on. He was exceptional at it, but he got cocky and took too many risks. In Tijuana, in 1986, a bull turned its head unexpectedly and Joe felt a horn enter his groin, severing his femoral artery. Surgeons worked on him for two hours and sewed him up with 176 stitches.

That was the end of Joe's career as a bull grabber. Instead, he turned to horses and mastered the art of el rejoneo, becoming such a gifted cavalier (a cavaleiro, to use the Portuguese word) that he expects someday to take the alternativa, a formal ceremony that would recognize his talent and establish him as a pro. He plans to do it in Portugal, where he has fought one time. He must have the approval of the promoters of the corrida and fight on a card with two full-fledged rejoneadores, alternating among the bulls. If he passes the test, he would be one of the first Americans to qualify, a feat that will mean as much to his father as it does to Joe himself.

The grand finale of the California bullfight season took place in Thornton. The four days of fights got under way on a Saturday afternoon, promptly at three o'clock, with the valley sun blazing and the temperature in the 90s. Two performers were on the card, both standouts imported from Portugal. Vitor Mendes, the headliner, had been a top-ranked matador on the tough Spanish circuit for many years, and he was renowned for his deft touch with the banderillas. For his star turn he would be paid about $23,000. Mendes shared the bill with Mario Miguel, an Azorean lad of twenty on the brink of international fame. Miguel was tall, slender, fair and blue-eyed—he was almost pretty, really—and he carried himself with the grace of a dancer.

The Azores Band, sprightly in its naval-style uniforms, marched into the ring to launch the festivities. Some sheriff's deputies on palominos came next, trailed by Mendes on foot with his cuadrilla, or assistants. Miguel, who would fight as a rejoneador, rode in on a glorious chestnut stallion. He wore tight breeches, a ruffled silk shirt and a knee-length coat of brocade, and when he raised an arm to salute the fans, he could have been a king surveying the peasantry.

El rejoneo originated with the upper classes as a way for a nobleman to prove his bravery and his skill on horseback, so a cavalier always fights first, before a matador. Miguel sat his stallion across from the corral and looked no more concerned than a man resting in his favorite easy chair. He didn't even blink when the bull was released. Its horns were not only shaved but also covered with a leather-and-steel glove to protect the horse, yet the charge was still fearsome. Miguel waited until the bull was almost upon him before he skipped away with a quick kick of his spurs.

The merry chase was on. Around and around they went, with Miguel teasing the bull and letting the horns nearly graze his saddle before he galloped on. Every narrow escape would boost his confidence, and he would push himself a little further, leaning back to brush the bull's massive head with his fingertips. His riding was fluid and exemplary. He could turn on a dime, and he placed three pairs of banderillas with amazing accuracy. When he was done, the forcados jumped in and subdued the weary bull, while Miguel took a lap around the ring to wild applause. He would be a hard act to follow, as Vitor Mendes surely knew. Mendes, alas, drew a terrible bull. The animal was clumsy and dull, so the matador, who was a veteran of such trials, did what he could to make things interesting. He offered exquisite capework at close range, for instance, but there were still problems. The bull kept stopping halfway through each pass, forcing Mendes to move even closer as he tried to produce a thrill. His frustration was evident, and perhaps it caused him to be careless, allowing the bull to lash out in a fury and catch him with a horn between his legs.

Down went Mendes in a heap. He lay motionless. The bull continued its attack, butting and trampling him until the cuadrilleros provided a distraction. A team of paramedics assisted Mendes to the sideline and tended to his injuries. This was the first sign that the damage wasn't serious. In a short time Mendes reappeared in the ring, as his code of honor dictated. His forehead was bruised, and he walked with a limp. He was determined to finish with a flourish, but his trousers were in tatters, and his genitals popped into view. Poor Mendes had to work the muleta while his nether parts flopped about in the open air. Some spectators laughed at his plight, but most were impressed by his nerve and tenacity, and they applauded him as loudly as they had Miguel.

On Monday, Joe Correia woke before dawn at the ranch in Madera and began preparing for the show in Thornton. He had a case of butterflies, as he usually did before a fight. "Let's go to Las Vegas," he joked, suggesting he'd rather be anywhere than in a bullring. He put in eight hours of honest toil before he left, making his own banderillas and grooming the three horses he'd ride, braiding their tails and threading ribbons through their manes until they looked ready for a parade. The drive north took another three hours. Joe pulled into town at twilight and dressed inside his father's RV. The surroundings were scarcely elegant, but he was upbeat. "I don't do this for the money," said Joe. He would earn about $2,500, a pittance compared to the fees of Mendes and Miguel.

Again the Azores Band struck up a paso doble, and Joe joined the formal procession into the ring. He did not ride Temperal, his favorite stallion, who is black and strong and has a stormy disposition. He chose a lesser mount instead, in case the bull inflicted harm. The first horse was his designated stalker, used to test the bull's fortitude and its mode of attack. Once Joe had established those factors, he would switch from stallion to stallion depending on his purpose, asking for speed or toughness or a superior ability to maneuver.

In the saddle Joe lacked the feathery finesse of Miguel. He was much older, thirty-three, and bigger and heavier, but he demonstrated the same fearlessness when his bull erupted from the corral. It was a decent bull for a change, too. The charge was straight and true, with no surprises. Joe spun his stallion with a sharp cry and forced the bull to pursue him. At the appropriate time he placed the banderillas with pinpoint accuracy, then followed with another pair as he worked dangerously close to the horns. He had just one disturbing moment. It came while he was basking in adulation, paying more attention to the crowd than to his job. The bull appeared to be defeated, gasping and dribbling urine, but all at once the animal roared back to life and crashed toward horse and rider. Only at the last instant did Joe wake up with a start, booting his stallion to safety. He grinned and shook his head, as though the mistake amused him—as though no one could ever learn all the lessons of the ring—and broke two banderillas in half, in a crowd-pleasing gesture that would force him to work still lower in the saddle and nearer the horns. The stunt went without a hitch, and Joe let the cheers wash over him. Astride his horse, he cut a heroic figure, his transformation complete. Manuel was happy for him, and Joe's mother, who'd been very anxious and had sometimes looked away from the action, was overjoyed. Her boy had survived! Joe stayed around to watch the other fights on the card and didn't load his van until midnight. He wasn't the slightest bit tired, though he knew he'd be exhausted the minute he hit the road. That was a small price to pay, because his good performance had moved him a step closer to his goal of the alternativa.

He would keep working at the ranch until then, schooling his horses and doing the usual chores. The Correias had a new crop of calves to brand, about 40 between six and eight months old. You might imagine that it would be a rough business to round them all up, scattered as they were over 516 acres, but Joe made it sound easy. "We'll be done before noon," he said, "unless somebody breaks out a jug of Portuguese red too early." This branding would be an auspicious one, because the date coincided with his father's sixtieth birthday, and if Manuel's luck continued to hold, the fates might yet present him with the brave bull of his dreams.

10
My Wicker Creel

I said goodbye to my oldest piece of fishing gear recently, a split-willow wicker creel I bought at Abercrombie & Fitch in San Francisco, believe it or not, in the days when the company still sold sporting goods and the concept of catch-and-release was in its infancy. I'd always been partial to Abercrombie because I grew up outside Manhattan and used to browse at the old flagship store on Madison Avenue when I was in my teens. The place was on a par with the Museum of Natural History, really, with an extraordinary—and ultimately depressing—display of big-game trophies, some shot by Teddy Roosevelt if I remember correctly, but it was the fly-casting pool on the roof of the building that knocked me out.

Not only the pool, though. For a budding angler, Abercrombie was a treasure chest of high-end equipment I knew even then I'd probably never be able to afford. As I watched the financial tyros and titans of industry browse among the Hardy reels and featherweight cane rods in preparation for a trip to the Test or the Itchen, or maybe a private preserve on the Beaverkill, I'd steal a glimpse at the pricetags and swoon. You could outfit yourself for a Kenyan safari, too, or, less exotically, replace the wickets for your croquet set or the blade of a good hunting knife. The store honestly lived up to its motto, "Where the Blazed Trail Crosses the Boulevard."

I've since read that Abercrombie carried about 48,000 flies and 16,000 lures on its sixth floor, the one devoted to angling. I was still a spin fisherman myself, partly because of my family's roots were in the lakes of Minnesota and Michigan, so I ignored the trays of Hare's Ears and Pale Morning Duns to sort through the Jitterbugs, Crazy Crawlers, and Hawaiian Wigglers. An instructor decked out in company-approved outdoor wear occupied a desk amid the surfeit of tackle, and if someone expressed an interest in a rod, he'd go over the fine points and escort the prospective buyer to the roof for a trial run. I never threw a cast myself, but I'm still haunted by the memory of the skillful men, and sometimes women, laying out their line high above the city, framed against a backdrop of skyscrapers.

At any rate, my creel was a spur-of-the-moment purchase. I bought it even before I owned a fly rod and saw it as a symbol of commitment to the goal of becoming a big-league angler. I felt proud to bring it home to my humble studio apartment in the Haight-Ashbury, where the druggies had burgled me twice in the past month and left me without a stereo or a TV. I had very little in the way of decorations, either, aside from a poster of Huey Newton and some psychedelia from the Fillmore West, so the creel soon landed in a prominent position on a vacant shelf. I seldom had time to fish due to my nine-to-five job, but I played with it at night in the absence of other forms of entertainment. I'd open the basket and imagine what it would be like to wrap a fat rainbow in ferns, as Hemingway had done in Spain.

One good thing about having a job, along with being able to afford a wicker creel and the rent on an apartment easily accessible to thieves, was that I got a two-week paid vacation. When I took mine that June, I had a new Fenwick fly rod in hand and thought I'd try the Merced River in Yosemite, not because I expected any superior fishing but for the sheer romance of it. If you're a native Californian, it may be difficult to understand how magesterial Half Dome looks to a flatlander from Long Island. I fell into Whitmanesque rhapsodies—Whitman also hailed from Long Island and called it Paumonauk after the Native American word for "fish-shaped"—when I first saw Bridalveil Falls, for instance, and I figured I'd hook a trout in the pool below.

My innocence, it seems, was boundless. It's true that Yosemite was a picnic then, compared to the congestion in the valley now, but I still hadn't counted on the vast number of Americans, not to mention tourists from around the world, who'd want to snap a photo of me. If you're a pro like those folks on Abercrombie's roof, it probably doesn't bother you when a newly affluent mobster from the Caucasus decides to include you in his montage, but I couldn't handle it, plus I had the damn creel slung over a shoulder to further inhibit me. When I finally caught a trout, it was far too small to even consider keeping.

I learned later how to fish the Merced the right way. First, you have to be willing to do some walking. It's tempting to plant yourself by one of the big pools as you enter the park—and they do hold some whopping trout—but they get hammered so hard that the effort isn't worth it. It's best to don your hiking boots and march away from the crowds. Fishing by day can be slow in Yosemite, although I've had a little luck with leeches and also streamers in dark colors, but late evening is usually the most profitable time during the summer, when both Caddis and PMDs in smaller sizes can work wonders. I've heard reports of 50-trout evenings, and though I'd be the last to accuse another angler of telling what Mark Twain, who spent the winter of 1864–65 in a Yosemite cabin, called "stretchers," I'd gladly settle for five nice ones myself.

With education comes enlightenment, of course, so I soon converted to the gospel of catch-and-release, although not before I put my creel to its proper use just once. It happened that same year when a friend and I headed for the Upper Sacramento over the Labor Day Weekend. We were still rookies and might have gone home skunked if we hadn't picked up some scuttlebutt at a café along the road, where a helpful stranger steered us to a stretch by Mossbrae Falls. Despite the holiday, we had lots of room to maneuver and the good fortune to bump into a massive hatch of Blue-Wing Olives. My friend hooked a fish after a half-dozen casts. It took me a while longer, but the wait proved worth it. The rainbow, as broad-bellied as a sumo wrestler, hadn't missed a meal all summer.

When I landed the fish, I searched briefly for ferns, but I had no success, so the bruiser went into the creel naked. I feel better about keeping the trout when I remember eating it for breakfast with some crispy pan-roasted potatoes and a pot of cowboy coffee, but only a *little* better. (I've since read that there's an official recipe for Hemingway Trout that involves coating the fish in a blend of lemon juice, parsley, green onions, and pepper, then rolling it in cornmeal and frying it in bacon grease.) Shortly after this adventure—or misadventure from the rainbow's point-of-view—I stuck to the catch-and-release pledge, thus making my creel obsolete.

That presented a problem, though. I'd grown fond of the creel. I liked the classy look of the wicker and how the leather had aged and developed a burnished patina. Instead of stuffing it into a closet, I chose to be inventive and devised a new use for it. At first, I turned it into a picnic basket and packed it with sandwiches and fruit, lugging it along the stream until a pal remarked on how heavy it must be. That explained the pain I'd been feeling in my left shoulder. Next I stored my extra flies in it, but the hooks got stuck between the wicker slats. After that I admitted defeat, and the creel reverted to being a decorative item, although I drew the line when a girlfriend tried to turn it into a planter full of nasturtiums and ivy.

For the past few years, the creel has languished in a San Anselmo storage locker while I've been living abroad, but when I last visited California I realized it might have some value to a collector, so I did a bit of research. Some antique creels are worth a small fortune, I learned, but not mine—it was too common. Apparently collectors prize much older types, such as those of Asian split willow imported from China and Japan to the west coast, where artisans added the leather touches. If you have any relatives in Oregon, ask them to check the basement for a creel made by George Lawrence of Portland, a firm that specialized in harnesses and saddles. A Lawrence creel from the 1920s in wicker and cowhide, size 2A, once commanded a price of $3,500.

Bill Lawrence, George's great grandson, retired from the family business not long ago, but he still crafts a few creels in his spare time. To judge by his website, they're extremely handsome and even come in colors from a rich sea-green to a super patriot's model in red, white, and blue. I assume they're too expensive to ever be employed in the field, but I wouldn't mind having one to admire as a work of art. As for my Abercrombie creel, I sold it at a garage sale before I left for Ireland again, but it wasn't easy to do. I suffered a tense moment, in fact, when a woman offered me ten bucks for it. It wasn't the money that put me off. I just suffered a sudden flashback and made her promise she wouldn't use it as a planter before I let her take it away.

11
Never Say Never: Ray "Boom Boom" Mancini's Last Fight

On a cold winter morning in Youngstown, Ohio, Ray "Boom Boom" Mancini, who'd once been the lightweight champion of the World Boxing Association, said goodbye to his mother and father and left home for Nevada to begin training for the most important fight of his career. His training camp was at the El Dorado Hotel, in downtown Reno, and when he arrived he found large cardboard cutouts of himself propped against the casino's slot machines. There were banners that read, "Welcome, Boom Boom!" and "The El Dorado Welcomes Ray Mancini!" and several pumped up gamblers gathered around to wish him luck. Mancini was used to such treatment from the fans. In boxing circles, he'd always been a big draw, and he knew how to smile and make small talk, and also how to accept a handshake without doing any damage to the fists that had helped to earn him almost six million dollars in purse money.

Mancini had an executive suite of rooms at the hotel, closed off from public view. Like most veteran boxers, he despised the discipline and routine of getting into shape, so he was glad to be meeting a boxer for whom he had a genuine dislike—Livingstone Bramble, a complex and worldly wise Rastafarian from the Virgin Islands. Bramble had taken away Mancini's title in Buffalo, New York in June of 1984. Mancini hadn't been himself that night. He'd felt sick and out of sorts, as if he were coming down with the flu. He thought Bramble had proved to be an unworthy champion. This had less to do with Bramble's acknowledged talent than with his behavior. He had insulted the Mancini family and done stupid things, like invoking voodoo curses and sparring with a chicken. These antics had grated against Mancini's love of the fight game, his respect for its rituals and institutions, and had stoked his desire for revenge.

He did his roadwork in the high desert country, running along paths that skirted the base of snowcapped mountains. He skipped rope, tossed around a medicine ball, and kept tabs on his weight. Almost every afternoon, he took on his sparring partners in a full-sized ring at the El Dorado. He was compactly build and thickly muscled. He had a broken nose and a scarred face, but he still dreamed of becoming an actor someday and making his mark in Hollywood. Among his pals he counted Playboy bunnies and movie stars. He knew Mickey Rourke and Sly Stallone. He knew Frankie Avalon well, and Avalon—he of the beach blanket franchise—had warned him that whenever you do a film you leave a chunk of your life behind. That made sense to Mancini. He was twenty-three years old, and his brief and sometimes tragic time in the ring was drawing to a close.

Mancini started his career as a pro in and around Youngstown. He advised the local reporters he was dedicating himself to winning a lightweight title in honor of his father, Lenny, the original "Boom Boom," who'd been a contender himself until he was wounded on a French battlefield during the Second World War. This made for good copy, and Mancini soon acquired a canny, ambitious manager, David Wolf, a former sportswriter who knew the value of a hot property. With Wolf guiding him, steering him clear of potentially dangerous opponents, Mancini followed a cautious route to the top, and in May, 1982, after a vicious defeat at the hands of Alexis Arguello, he beat a shopworn fighter, Arturo Frias, and became the WBA champ.

Mancini was still handsome and relatively unmarked in those days, and his outgoing personality made him a favorite with the fans. He was white, Italian, and eminently marketable. The television networks recognized his crossover appeal; he attracted both men and women viewers. He'd never been a stylish boxer; there was little art to his hooks or jabs. He'd won twenty-three of his twenty-four pro bouts simply by giving better than he got, by being more daring and courageous than his opponents, but his flailing approach had cost him dearly. In swarming over other boxers, he'd left himself open to blows, and he'd been hit more often, and with better shots, than less aggressive fighters.

He earned his first title defense in November, 1983 against the South Korean Duk Koo Kim in a match CBS televised.

There were more deserving lightweights around, but Wolf, on Mancini's behalf, declined to tackle them. Duk Koo Kim was a mystery man. Though the WBA ranked him first in his division, he'd never fought in the United States and spoke no English. Apparently he saw himself as a warrior going to battle, defending the flag of his nation. On a lampshade in his hotel room, he'd scrawled "Kill or be killed." In the ring, he turned out to be a fierce but unskilled brawler, and he survived through thirteen brutal rounds before Mancini decked him. Duk Koo Kim did not get up from the canvas, nor did he ever regain consciousness. He died of a cerebral hemorrhage in a Las Vegas hospital, and his mother donated his vital organs to science. A month later, still distraught, she died herself after drinking a bottle of poison.

In the annals of boxing, there's an ample history of accidental death, but Mancini is a sensitive man, and the passing of Duk Koo Kim left him devastated. A devout Catholic, he spent months consulting his family and his parish priest before deciding to step into the ring again. He acquitted himself fairly well in four subsequent bouts, including a promotional one in Italy, but then he came up against Livingstone Bramble, who—unlike Mancini—had risen through the ranks without a management team to help him. Mancini was a heavy favorite to win their fight, but Bramble surprised him. He's a wicked counterpuncher, and he sliced through Mancini's haphazard attack and took him apart. Mancini bled so badly from cuts around his eyes the bout had to be stopped in the fourteenth round. He spent the night in a Buffalo hospital under observation, with lacerations in both eyelids. One required eight stitches to close; the other required six.

Mancini had endured such a beating his intimates worried about his health. The promoter Bob Arum, who'd worked with him, stated publicly that Ray should retire, and some other insiders agreed. Mancini was rich and famous, and he had no compelling reason to go on. He'd achieved his goal of becoming a champ, after all. Anyone could see he wasn't giving as good as he got anymore. HBO had done a computer analysis of the Bramble bout, and it showed Mancini had thrown an amazing fourteen hundred and eight punches—more than a hundred per round, an enormous expenditure of energy. But he'd landed only three hundred and thirty-eight of them, or twenty-four per cent, whereas Bramble scored with a whopping fifty-three per cent of his shots. In spite of the disparity—and the beating—Mancini demanded a rematch. He couldn't cope with being a loser. Already his market value was in decline. A publishing company shelved his autobiography, and a major magazine, perhaps Sports Illustrated, had cancelled its plans for a profile.

The idea of a rematch was catnip to Bramble and his manager, Lou Duva. Mancini, though battered, still had a marquee name, and that would insure the fight would be sold to television. (Without the money and legitimacy television grants, boxing couldn't continue as a major sport.) Bramble, on his own, held no fascination for the networks. His only fans were reggae lovers, fellow rastas, folks from the Virgin Islands, and those who habitually root for outsiders. Advertisers would find it hard to be enthusiastic about a worshipper of

Hailie Selassie who wore dreadlocks and identified with the oppressed of the world. Moreover, Bramble's boxing style was too subtle for the medium. He was a defensive type, calculating and intelligent, and he seldom got into any trouble—no blood and no gore. To appreciate him, a viewer needed to understand boxing as an intricate contest, not a spectacle. On the other hand, Mancini worked in broad strokes. Nonstop action was his métier, and his walloping delivery was ideal for an audience used to watching car crashes and cops chase junkies through the streets of Miami.

Once Mancini signed on the dotted line, he had to be accommodated in certain ways. According to a WBA rule, a rematch can't be sanctioned unless each boxer has fought somebody else in the interim—this prevents a boxer from taking a dive in exchange for a guaranteed second chance. Bramble had fought Edwin Curet; the rule was waived for Mancini. In the WBA rankings, Mancini was only third, so Tyrone Crawley, the No. 1 contender, had to be paid off to step aside. Crawley earned a sweet hundred and fifty thousand, plus a contract to fight the winner. To resolve the concern about Mancini's condition, Dave Wolf distributed a packet of testimonials from private physicians that described the positive results of many neurological exams. In the summer of 1984, Mancini underwent a CAT scan, and Dr. Jeffrey Schwartz, a Manhattan orthopedic surgeon and his chief medical adviser, saw no disturbing changes or irregularities in his brain tissue.

But Dr. Schwartz was not so sanguine about the delicate skin around his patient's eyes. The skin was so fragile Mancini suffered subcutaneous cuts whenever he did any sparring, and those cuts were primed to burst to the surface by the time the actual fight rolled around—just as they'd done in Buffalo. He advised Ray to wear a protective mask he trained, but Mancini refused to do so, fearing that the onlookers and the media would interpret it as a sign of weakness.

The WBA chose Reno for the fight. More and more championships are being held in Nevada because casino owners willingly contribute to the lavish site-selection fees the alphabet organizations insist upon. But that was no hardship for the casinos. Indeed, the city fathers of Reno estimated that five million dollars in ancillary profits would spill over to local businesses, much of it in the proceeds from gambling. To promote the match, the WBA chose Dan Duva, Lou's son, and his company, Main Events. Duva shopped around the live-broadcast rights and sold them to HBO for more than a million. That put the promotion in the black before a punch was thrown, and Duva agreed to pay each boxer about three-quarters of a million. It was unusual for a challenger— Mancini—to get as much as a champ, but in boxing no point of reference is ever absolute.

A big-money fight always stirs up a gambling town, so Reno was delighted to play host to Ray Mancini. His supporters began to fly in a few days ahead and took advantage of the package deals at various casinos. Among them were hometown boys from Ohio, high rollers in spring pastels, and bottle blonds in clingy off-brand jeans, and they convened at the El Dorado almost every day to watch the dethroned champ sweat. Both

Mancini and his trainer, a fierce-looking guy called Murphy Griffith, whose shaved head was most often hidden beneath a Yankees cap, felt he'd overdone it while training for the first Bramble tilt, losing his edge in the gym, and they monitored his progress closely, hoping he'd peak at the right moment. The loyalists were banking on this, backing Mancini heavily even though he was a three-to-one underdog. "Boom Boom!" they shouted or, more pointedly, "Whip the freak!"

The last press conference took place on a balmy afternoon in mid-February, 1985. Mancini arrived a few minutes before Bramble. Dressed casually, with his longish black hair combed back in an airy pompadour, he strolled in with some other young men of approximately the same size, his sparring partners. The looked like members of a Police Athletic League boxing club, clean-cut kids from the suburbs. The press-kit photos of Mancini dated from prior to the Frias bout, so it was disconcerting to see how much his face had changed since then. His nose was broader, more splayed, and the skin over his cheekbones was stretched tight, as if it had no give left in it. Only his charm was still intact. He was warm, open, and modest. When he smiled his eyes flashed in their abused sockets, and the joy he took in his trade was manifest. He was glad to be a boxer, willing to accept the grueling dictates of the game, and the reporters admired him for that and acted as though he, not Bramble, held the crown.

"You going to retire after this one, Ray?" somebody asked.

Mancini shrugged it off. "I don't make predictions."

Livingstone Bramble finally entered and sat at the other end of a long table, playing a street tough to hype the bout.

He understood the age-old ring drama of white against black, good against evil, and he handled the villain's role with finesse. In his sunglasses and his Bramble brim, a flat, multicolored pancake of a hat, he brooded on cue and pretended to cast a juju spell on his opponent. He presented Mancini with a ceramic skull (made in Taiwan) and produced a voodoo doll from a little sack, then stuck some pins in it.

"Your eyes jumping around yet, Ray?" he wondered. "I told you I'd do anything to win."

Bramble seemed to have no sense he'd crossed an invisible border into the land of bad taste. Nobody knew what to make of him, not even his manager. He had a capacity for reinventing himself, baffling the audience with his jive.

He'd been invited to train at the MGM Grand Hotel, a monolith out in the desert that had once burned down in a fire, dealing its occupants the ultimate bad hand, and he was driving the security force crazy. He strolled through the casino at all hours with his pet boa constrictor draped around his neck, relishing in the fact he was pulling off a stunt no other black dude was ever likely to duplicate. The MGM's trademark lion, caged on a lower level of the hotel, caught a whiff of the snake one night and reverted to jungle genotype, roaring and flaring its nostrils, but that was no skin off Bramble's back. He took a carpe diem attitude toward being the champ, enjoying it while he could.

If Bramble seemed relaxed around the Grand, he had some secret worries. As an amateur he'd never won a rematch, and he thought he might be jinxed. He was pissed off at Dave Wolf because Wolf kept insinuating Bramble and his entourage, who wore Bramble brims, black satin warm-up jackets, and shades indoors, were using drugs. Lou Duva was also steamed about the accusation, and he countered by suggesting Mancini's corner was much more likely to rely on an illegal substance—Monsole's solution in this case, a banned medication that can close a cut in an instant. (If Monsole's dribbles into a fighter's eye, though, it can blind him.) In a pact forged at a WBA rules meeting, Duva and Wolf agreed that their boxers would submit to a urinalysis after the match.

In addition, Bramble was upset about how the press was treating him. He was sick of hearing how wonderful Mancini was, how Mancini embodied all the traditional (and wonderful) virtues of white America. All Rastafarians know themselves to be laboring under the weight of Babylon culture, and one night, as Bramble stood outside the Grand, waiting for a parking attendant to fetch his car—it was lost somewhere in the lot—so he could go out for a vegetarian dinner, he spoke of his dismay.

"It's always the same, man," he sighed. "Everybody telling you what to do. You know what I'm getting for this fight? Seven hundred fifty thousand. Mancini, I bet he's getting more. You call that justice? Boxing, it ain't never going to change."

In the last days before the fight, Bramble vanished from sight, possibly gone off to some spectral chamber to replenish his juices, but Mancini continued to put on a show at the El Dorado. The crowd attending his final workout was larger than ever, and they howled when he bopped in to a Hall & Oates tune blaring from a ghetto-blaster. He took off his robe, climbed into the ring, and did some calisthenics at top speed. He was in superb condition, his legs solid and his stomach trim and flat. The match was fast approaching, so he didn't spar to protect his hands from injury, but he laced on the gloves anyway and tossed a flurry of rights and lefts at the padded mitts Murphy Griffith held up as targets. His hooks were powerful given his low center of gravity, but his jabs lacked any snap and might have no effect on Bramble, whose head was reputed to be as hard as a coconut.

While Mancini danced around the ring, Fabulous Ford Jennings, a sparring partner, observed from a distance and warily unwrapped the tape from his fists. He'd run through a set of exercises, too, doing sit-ups and pushups and pounding a heavy bag. This was the fourth time Fabulous Ford had been hired to train with a champ, and the trappings of stardom no longer thrilled him. Sick of living in a hotel room, he talked wistfully about Fort Worth, his hometown, where he'd turned pro at the age of eighteen.

"I'll tell you this, I don't ever want to see no more slot machines or craps tables," he complained, letting the tape fall from his fingers in thick ribbons. "You know what I'd rather see? Cows, pastures, and cracked old streets. I'd like to see some nature. That's what I'd rather see."

Jennings claimed to have started boxing when he was seven and swore he'd been hit—really hit—just once in his twenty pro bouts. If you asked him where, he pointed to a scar over an eye and boasted that he hadn't needed any stitches, only a damn butterfly bandage to close the wound. Mancini hadn't been able to touch him, he said, but sparring partners invariably believe they can outfox their employers. Maybe Jennings was trying to boost his confidence. He hadn't fought for ten months, and he was eager for a payday. He blamed "manager problems" as boxers often do, and swore he'd written the Texas State Athletic Commission about his plight.

That evening, after a shower and a change of clothes, Jennings set up shop at an upstairs hotel bar, adorned in copious gold chains around his neck and making himself available to any feminine fringe benefits that might pass his way. His roommate, Raymond Reyes, another sparring partner, sat with him. Reyes, an intelligent young New York Puerto Rican, had fought very little. He spoke in complex sentences and desired to present himself as a "well-rounded person," because he figured it would enhance his chances of being interviewed on TV. Nobody cared to interview a boxer who couldn't talk right, he believed.

Reyes had fought three times in the Golden Gloves at Madison Square Garden and had lost each bout, but he felt older and wiser now, a seasoned pro. The boxer he most admired was Hector "Macho" Camacho, who'd had manager problems and problems with marijuana. In Camacho he recognized an attractive blend of bling and bravado. Reyes counted himself an aware person, somebody who understood the risks of the fight game. He'd seen punch-drunk guys around the gym, and he intended to retire when he was twenty-eight or twenty-nine, before his own brain turned to mush. He was having a good time in Reno, maybe the time of his life, and he wanted to let his dream stretch out for as long as he could.

In the literature of boxing, and in the movies, the punch-drunk fighter is a stock character. His speech is slurred; his memory's impaired; he walks with a stagger or on his heels; and his perceptual motor ability is severely diminished. In medical terms, the syndrome is known as dementia pugilistica. Scientists in Great Britain began to investigate it more than thirty years ago and soon amassed incontrovertible evidence most former boxers were afflicted to some degree. This prompted the editors of The Lancet, the principal British journal of medicine, to declare in 1959 that the medical case against boxing was so strong they were forced to lobby for its abolition. They didn't make much headway. Boxing is still quite popular throughout the United Kingdom.

In the U.S., there'd been little research into the debilitating effects of boxing until recently when the Journal of the American Medical Association started publishing editorials and papers that constituted an all-out assault on the sport. Dr. George Lundberg, the Journal's editor, contended boxing is as medically unsound as smoking or heavy drinking. Its sole purpose was for one man to inflict injury on another, and on that basis alone, he recommended, it should be banned. The editorials sparked an uproar, and Lundberg received irate letters from pro-boxing colleagues, who accused him of trying to deprive boxers of their rights in a free society. None of the correspondents took issue with the scientific data however; it was as convincing as it had been abroad.

Of the research papers published in the Journal, the most incriminating is "Brain Damage in Modern Boxers." A team of New York doctors give an account in it of how they discovered unequivocal signs of cerebral dysfunction in eighty-seven per cent of the pros they studied. The sample was admittedly small, being made up of eighteen volunteers—thirteen former boxers, three active ones, and three active Golden Glovers. The former pros were between twenty-five and sixty years old. They hadn't quit for medical, neurological, or psychological reasons, and they had no known history of drug or alcohol abuse. They'd had, on average, a total of eighty-three amateur and pro bouts apiece. The average number of pro bouts was twenty-nine. Only one pro was a slugger like Mancini. The others were artful dodgers, who practiced self-defense.

The subjects submitted to a battery of neurological tests including an EEG and a CAT scan. The Golden Glovers, who'd fought about as often as Raymond Reyes, had no measurable brain damage, although there were indications of subtle brain injury. Thirteen of the fifteen pros had abnormal results. They suffered from a variety of complaints such as disorientation, confusion, temporary amnesia, and Parkinsonian disturbance. The doctors noted that the subjects were successful boxers, not tomato cans. Among them were two world champs, two Golden Gloves champs, a Pan American Games champ, and three ranked contenders. These men could take a punch. In their four hundred and sixteen fights, they'd been knocked out just sixteen times.

The paper wasn't definitive, but its implications were serious for the sport. Brain damage was not the result of a single hard knockout punch, as some boxers believed; it appeared instead to be related to the amount of time a fighter spent in the ring and the amount of punishment he absorbed.

Nor was brain damage confined to professionals; it turned up among the amateurs, too. One active pro had fought only once for a purse, but he'd already developed a cavum septum pellucidum—a cave, or tear, in the membrane separating the lobes of the brain. He'd had thirty-four amateur bouts, though, and countless hours of sparring. Furthermore, brain damage appeared to be widespread among fighters. Its early stages were often undetectable, except with expensive, sophisticated technology like a CAT scan. Worse still, the condition was degenerative, and the symptoms often didn't materialize for years.

"The cumulative effect of multiple subconcussive blows is a likely etiology," the doctors concluded. In response to their work, the AMA adopted a resolution that stated in part, "Despite some positive aspects of the sport, the American public is best served by strong AMA opposition to boxing at all levels."

The Lawlor Events Center, at the University of Nevada, was filled almost to capacity for the Reno Rematch. Dan Duva put the crowd at about twelve thousand and the gate at about eight hundred thousand dollars. A ringside seat went for two hundred bucks, and they were occupied by the WBA brass, local politicians, media freeloaders, lounge comedians, showgirls, aspiring showgirls, and showgirls who'd fallen on hard times and were turning tricks. A few cowboys from the range wandered around half-blasted, done in by many reloads of whiskey at a bar decorated with dead, stuffed animals—bighorn sheep, a water buffalo—in museum quality glass cases.

There were six bouts on the undercard at Lawlor. They represented the nether world of boxing, where chosen fighters are "built up" for the big time. In these matches, young boxers whose potential and looks, style, or race might appeal to the TV honchos mop the floor with over-the-hill journeymen—or bums to put it less politely. The bums have no union to support them as other athletes do, so they fight for whatever the traffic will bear. They have no medical benefits or pension plan. Their job is to travel from state to state and get knocked out, usually in a round or two. They take the same risks as a champ does, but they do it for peanuts.

Dave Wolf managed two boxers on the undercard. In order to sign Mancini, Dan Duva was forced to sign them as well, and to find them opponents and feature their pictures in the fight program. Wolf had the right to approve the opponents—every manager does—and he considered himself an excellent judge of who might be appropriate as the fall guy. In his six and a half years in the game, his charges had lost only seven times.

For Luis Espinosa, a junior lightweight, Wolf approved Juan "El Tigre" Romero, who'd lost a third of his bouts. Espinosa worked over Romero, hitting him so frequently that when Romero finally went down in the fifth, he waved a bright red glove and shouted, "No mas! No mas!" For Donny Poole, a Canadian welterweight, Wolf settled on Chino Bermudez, a tall, flabby man in his thirties whose face had an Asian cast. Bermudez hailed form either Los Angeles or Tijuana—he used addresses in both places—and he'd had seventy-four *recorded* pro bouts. In his youth he'd been a winner, but now he lost consistently. He'd arrived in Reno just before the fight, and when he weighed in, attired in the shabby clothes of a field hand, he proved to be ten pounds overweight. He looked awful then, but in the ring he looked even worse, downright implausible. On occasion he did something well, drawing on memory, but Poole hit him at will, and he went down in the second, swooning, and then twice more in the third before the ref ended it.

Dan Duva later claimed he couldn't do much about the situation. Managers wouldn't let a hot prospect take a chance on getting beat, not unless the money was right. As for Wolf, he didn't believe the bouts were mismatches. In his biased opinion, Romero was a decent boxer, and Bermudez, a "wily veteran," had actually taught Donny Poole a few valuable lessons. Besides, there was a budget involved. Romero was part of a cheap package deal out of Phoenix, which also included Tony Cisneros, another knockout victim. Jerry Lewis (twelve wins, thirteen losses) wasn't part of the package. Vince Dunfee decked him, and Lewis went home to California and got word his license to fight in that state wouldn't be renewed. Chino Bermudez heard the same and ambled off to Mexico.

Ray Mancini, wearing a regal red silk robe, paraded into the arena throwing punches and kisses. The crowd, mostly white, rose as a body to cheer when he slipped through the ropes. Moments later, Bramble made his entrance to Bob Marley's "Buffalo Soldier," a reggae song about black men conscripted into the Union Army and ordered to kill Indians. "I'm just a Buffalo soldier fighting for survival," Marley sang, and Bramble, in black trunks bearing a yellow skull-and-crossbones, danced in the ring, his eyes closed, while in a front row his fans from the Virgin Islands held aloft his infant son. Bramble's dreadlocks were slick with Vaseline, as were his nose and cheeks. The crowd booed him, but he'd expected as much. "In America," he once said, "if you're different they say you're strange."

The fight started briskly. Mancini came out of his corner smoking and attacked Bramble, whose height advantage and superior reach—he had several inches on the challenger—made things difficult. But Mancini compensated, as always, with courage and daring. He stood toe-to-toe with the taller man and took three punches to land one. Bramble scored points throughout these exchanges, refusing to brawl. Instead he waited patiently and looked for openings in his opponent's defense. When he threw a jab he did so with authority, in clockwork fashion, often targeting the eyes. Mancini was honed as sharp as could be, but his scar tissue and those subcutaneous cuts soon betrayed him. In the second round, Bramble sliced open his right eyelid; the skin around his left eye began to swell and turn red. Then, in the fifth, Bramble opened another cut, this an inch-long gash near the left lid, and blood flowed down Mancini's cheek, as if he'd been slashed with a razor.

Through sheer willpower, Mancini kept himself together. He had a fine sixth round, wiping away the blood with his gloves and slowing Bramble with a series of efficient hooks to the body, but Bramble redoubled his efforts in the seventh, concentrating on Mancini's eyes, jabbing at them, widening the cuts. When Mancini returned to his corner at the bell, ringsiders heard him gripe, "I can't see." His cut man, Paul Percifield, closed the wounds as best he could, but Bramble opened them again in the eighth, and the ref called in the attending physician, Dr. Charles Filippini, and sought a medical opinion about whether or not Mancini should continue.

Dr. Filippini is a GP in Reno. He earned a pittance for his job and viewed it as he might a community service. He'd presided at many fights including four world championships, but he'd stopped only one. He was aware of his difficult position. Millions of dollars were riding on Mancini, and his backers were desperate for him to finish, hoping for a knockout since he appeared to be behind on points. Filippini also knew most boxing people mistrust doctors, and he wasn't sure how Mancini's corner would react. At other fights he'd been blocked from examining an injury, elbowed aside by infuriated trainers. "They just want us around to pick up the pieces," he later remarked.

He'd given pre-fight physicals to all the boxers on the card, but the exams were cursory, and he wished he had the wherewithal to be more thorough. He'd read the AMA research, and it worried him. He believed every boxer should have a CAT scan at the start of his career and then after every bout to alert him to any alteration in his brain tissue. But CAT scans are costly, and Filippini had no idea where that kind of money might come from, except perhaps from the TV networks. He leaned over the ropes, pried open Mancini's closed eye with his fingers, and peered into the bloody socket, determining that Boom Boom's eyelids weren't split and his retinas weren't detached. In essence, the cuts were a soft-tissue trauma. They might look terrible and impair Mancini's vision to a degree, but they'd do no permanent harm.

So Mancini fought on. But the match wasn't the same anymore—it didn't seem clean or fair. Now a man with a handicap was pitted against a better boxer in his prime. Mancini's talent and bravery were undeniable, but his body had let him down. As he circled the ring, flicking the blood from his eyes with his gloves, he brought to mind many other champs in the dismal last stages of their careers. There was something very moving and very sad about his relentless pursuit of Bramble, something that went to the root of boxing's problems. It was a sport that did not know where to draw the line. The line, such as it was, kept shifting, subject to crude economies—to the whims of the networks, the alphabet boys, the promoters and managers, and all the other vested interests in control. On this point the record was clear—only rarely did a fighter quit the game before it was too late.

Because Mancini had a touch of greatness, he landed punches, even good punches, but the blood still flowed. It spotted his chest and speckled his shoulders and back. Bramble later admitted he was distressed by the sight. If the eyes were his, he'd had have thrown in the towel and return to the ring another day. Most boxers don't enjoy inflicting unnecessary punishment, but Bramble had no choice. He'd hammered Mancini the same way in their first bout, yet he'd been behind on all three judges' scorecards. So Bramble went about his business and poked the eyes. He punched Mancini six hundred and seventy-four times in all; two hundred and fifty-five of those punches struck Mancini in the face. When he was hit on the jaw or the side of his head, his soft brain swirled and glided within his skull, imperiling blood vessels and nerve endings. His future as a person with charm and charisma—his future as a human being—was at risk.

Mercifully the fight ended. Among most reporters who'd kept score, Bramble was an easy winner, ahead by three or four points, although a few dissenters awarded the laurels to Mancini. The judges, too, scored in favor of Bramble, but only by a point on each card. The HBO computer analysis showed that Mancini had connected with just twenty-eight per cent of his shots; Bramble was almost twice as accurate at fifty-five per cent. Once again Mancini had lost decisively, but that seemed not to matter to him. He took pride in having survived. When he met the press he delivered a non-stop monologue fueled by a mixture of oxygen and adrenaline. He wore a maroon towel over his head like a burnoose, and his left eye was purple and nearly shut.

"I hope I've been good for boxing," he offered humbly. "I tried."

A reporter asked if he were hurting.

"I'm not going to lie and say I'm not," Mancini replied. "But to what extent?"

Lenny Mancini—broken nose, a shock of white hair—sat next to his son, and somebody wondered if he wanted Ray to keep fighting.

"If it was me, I'd say forget about it," Lenny told the media.

"He always says that." Boom Boom grinned at his old man. "I'm his baby."

Another reporter asked if Mancini planned to retire now. "I've got to think about it. To thine own self be true," he countered. "You guys didn't know I can quote Shakespeare, did you?"

He laughed and invited everybody to a big bash at the El Dorado, though he didn't attend it. Instead he went off to the hospital, where the doctors sewed up the wounds in his eyelids and around his eyes with twenty-seven stitches. By midnight, he was in his suite, eating a dish of chocolate ice cream.

In the morning, at the MGM Grand, Bramble, still casual in jeans and a Bramble brim, anointed himself the lightweight champion of the universe. When he was asked why he'd seldom used his right hand during the fight, he claimed it was because his right glove hadn't come from the belly part of the cow.

"Are you going to honor your contract with Tyrone Crawley?"

Bramble kept quiet. He'd leave that up to his manager. The chump he really hoped to fight was Hector Camacho, who'd been at ringside in a gold lame suit and rhinestone-studded sunglasses. WBA rankings aside, Camacho as an opponent would generate a significant chunk of change.

Lou Duva jumped in to make the case against Crawley. He had the sort of mug you see on 1940s movie cops; all he needed was a fedora to double for Broderick Crawford.

"With Crawley you get a stinking fighter," Duva maintained. "I don't like a Crawley fight. There's nothing good about him stylewise. It would just stink out the joint."

He meants Crawley's style was similar to Bramble's and might give his fighter fits. He also meant Crawley was a nobody to the networks and might not sell to television.

Bramble preened, but his moment of glory was short-lived. The full weight of Babylon culture soon crashed down on him. The post-fight urinalysis revealed a banned substance in his urine—ephedrine, a crystalline alkaloid commonly used for the relief of hay fever, asthma, and nasal congestion. In large doses or injected intramuscularly, it elevates blood pressure and works as a stimulant. At first Bramble couldn't figure how it had gotten into his system. He was a vegetarian, a true health freak, and avoided chemicals of any kind. But he did swallow a capsule of Chi Power daily, a supposedly Chinese herbal concoction. Chi Power turned out to contain Ma Huang, or Ephedra sinica. The Nevada Athletic Commission fined Bramble fifteen thousand dollars.

Then his tilt against Hector Camacho failed to materialize. The Crawley fight was scheduled instead per the WBA's insistence, but Bramble broke a hand in training, and NBC cancelled its contract. When it was rescheduled, Crawley injured himself, and NBC again dropped out. Many months dragged by, and Bramble, a king without a kingdom, became so depressed he was thinking about moving to Montana and buying a cattle ranch—dreadlocks on horseback, Chi Power in the saddle. Eventually, though, Bramble fought and defeated Crawley in another impressive performance. But on other fronts there were new problems. He'd fired Lou Duva, and Duva was suing him for a share of his purse.

In the weeks following the match, Ray Mancini took it easy. For the first time in five years, he let his body rest— no training, no nothing. When CBS ran a videotape of the fight, he appeared on camera live, without Bramble, and put forth through his puffy lips a revised version of the night in question. Now he felt certain he'd won convincingly, and that Bramble's "drug use," however accidental, ought to cost him the title.

In New York, Dr. Schwartz examined Mancini again and informed him that his cuts would be fully healed in a few months. So Boom Boom flew to Florida to play some golf and conduct an inner debate about the possibility of retiring. Every few days, he phoned Dave Wolf to check on any fight offers. There were plenty, all for big bucks. Mancini was still white and still popular. Would he be able to turn down a million dollars to gain five pounds and tackle a leading junior welterweight? Mancini wasn't sure. How many people could refuse a million for taking a pounding? And it wasn't really the pounding that bothered Boom Boom—he blanched at the idea of going through another training camp. He was tired of paying his dues and, besides, he had other options.

The William Morris Agency had signed him to a contract, so he decided to move to Los Angeles. He bought a house and relaxed around the pool. His actor pals understood his quandary and how a million-dollar deal messes with your head. One day, maybe out of habit, he started working out in a gym at Mickey Rourke's place. He took it slowly, testing himself, but he just couldn't handle it anymore. He'd had it with the sacrifice and the pain, and called a press conference to announce his retirement. Instead he'd roll the dice and try his luck in Hollywood. Probably he'd never be a great thespian, he realized, but he thought he could do Rambo-type roles. He believed he could make a go of it, although he wouldn't rule out the chance that in the future, if the circumstances were right, he might return to the ring.

"One thing I've learned," Mancini explained. "Never say never."

12
The Mayflies
of Lough Arrow

It was Tennessee Williams' Blanche DuBois who depended on the kindness of strangers, and that's how I felt when I moved to Ireland to be with the woman who's now my wife. I packed some flies, a reel, and a nine-foot, four-piece fly rod, but the only trout stream near her house in Dublin is the Dodder River, a pretty little tributary of the Liffey. It's difficult to fish, partly because the wild browns it holds are spooky, but also because it flows through an urban park where the dog walkers let their mutts go splashing.

So I was excited to be invited to try my hand on Lough Arrow, a beautiful limestone lake in County Sligo famous for its mayfly hatches. It came through the offices of a friend, who put me in touch with Barrie Cooke, one of Ireland's finest painters and a fly fisher par excellence. Cooke lived on a remote two-acre spread above the lough, not far from the tiny village of Kilmactranny that consists entirely of a pub and a gas pump. Outside the pub stands a cast-iron statue of an angler, his rod bowed as he played a fish.

Cooke had just turned seventy. He was a robust, friendly, bearded man, whose round bifocals lent his eyes a quizzical look. His house was strewn with fishing books and magazines, and a taxidermied brown trout in a trophy case held pride of place. The Earl of Kensington had caught it on a dry fly in 1915, and it weighed seven pounds, four ounces. (One of Barrie's most celebrated paintings is "Lough Derg Pike," a lifesize portrait of the five-foot-long monster in question. Like the Earl's trout, he found the pike displayed in a pub.) Even the studio where he paints showed his devotion to angling, with several rods rigged up and at the ready and a pair of binoculars handy to keep an eye out for any hatches. He could be on the lough in less than five minutes.

Over a lunch of homemade carrot soup, cheese, bread, and white wine, Cooke told me about himself. He'd been born in England, spent his teens in Bermuda, and enrolled at Harvard to study marine biology, but he couldn't handle all the science involved, and after a course in art history he decided to paint instead, eventually studying with Oscar Kokoschka in Austria. In his early twenties, he took a ferry to Ireland and never looked back. He found a derelict shack to rent in County Clare in the Burren, a rocky isolated region of the west, where he could fish for trout, salmon, and pike. There he lived, as his friend Seamus Heaney put it, "like Huck Finn," snaring rabbits and shooting birds to stock his larder.

Barrie described himself as a romantic. He meant that in the sense of J.M.W. Turner, who was also a keen angler and believed in empathy. For Cooke empathy meant "living in something till your Self is forgotten," or the ability to be totally immersed in a painting (or a river) to the exclusion of everything else. Throughout his adult life, he'd honored that idea. He'd done nothing but paint and fish—no jobs, no teaching, and plenty of poverty until his work began to sell. He showed me some recent canvases. The paintings were abstract, although the forms were vaguely recognizable and brilliantly colored. Water figured as a primary element, and they all evidenced a deep bond with the natural world.

I returned the next day to go fishing. I brought along an assortment of standard California mayfly imitations such as the Parachute Adams and the March Brown, and Barrie gave me a few Lough Arrow Greens in sizes 16–20. It was early May, and he warned me that it was still a couple of weeks before the peak season. The fishing hadn't been great for the last two or three years, he added, because the Forestry Department had put down some rock phosphate fertilizer in wet weather. The phosphate washed into the lough and caused an algae bloom. Cooke had lately done some paintings of the bloom, finding it perversely engaging. His dealer wasn't happy. It's tough to market a painting called, "Algae Bloom, Lough Arrow."

He kept a rowboat in a cove below the house, fitted with an electric motor. The morning was very still and the weather perfect, with a gray sky and a light drizzle of rain. I saw signs of the algae bloom and understood Barrie's fascination. As viewed through a painter's eye, the colors were striking, often quite stunning. In the shallows of the lough, where coots were nosing about, reeds grew in profusion. Farther out, swans glided around, a trail of feathers in their wake. The trees were leafing out in a dozen shades of green, and we could hear the distant, skittery cry of grebes. Four small islands dotted the horizon, with low lying hills beyond them.

Cooke fired up the motor and off we went. As someone accustomed to crowded lakes and streams, I couldn't believe that we were the only boat on the water. True, it was a weekday, but still. I felt lucky to be there. Barrie guided us to a sort of inlet, then anchored. Nothing much was going on in terms of a hatch, although a few spent flies drifted by. I wished we'd packed some of the paperback mysteries that Cooke liked to read in the studio while waiting for some inspiration. But after twiddling our thumbs for a half-hour, a mayfly finally took wing.

Soon the air was filled with insects, including some lovely little Lake Olives with their long wispy tails. It wasn't what Barrie would call a prolific hatch compared to the old days, but I was impressed. The only problem was that the trout, all wild browns, weren't actively feeding. Rises happened so infrequently that I was casting blind in effect, and the lack of a breeze to ruffle the water meant each presentation had to be nearly perfect. That didn't bother Cooke. Every fly he cast landed as lightly as a speck of dust. He was an utter master.

When you know a lake or stream well, you tend to read it instinctively, and so it was with Barrie. He anticipated rises before they occurred, while I had to scan the water for dimples or other telltale signs. He hooked his first trout long before noon, a brown of about fourteen inches, broad and chunky. The average Lough Arrow brown weighs a pound or so, and this fish fit the bill. Cooke released it and quickly picked up another, again the same size. Envy was getting the best of me, and I rushed my casts and made a hash of things. Only when I took a deep breath, relaxed, and concentrated did I put a Lough Arrow Green into the ring of a rise and catch a fish.

Obviously, I had much to learn about Irish lough angling, so I was delighted when my host suggested we try the Unshin River the next morning. It's a limestone stream, deep and slow-moving, that flows out of Lough Arrow and weeds up in the summer. But in early May it was in fine shape and reminded me of the meadow stretches of Hat Creek. I'm far better on a stream than I am with stillwater, and I caught a handful of small browns on both dries and a Hare's Ear nymph. Even so, I spent half the time marveling at Barrie. At seventy, he still waded like a reckless teenager and could lay out fifty feet of line with pinpoint accuracy.

That night, we dropped in at the Bow and Arrow, the village pub. It was just a single large room in a house that was centuries old. A turf fire roared against the chill of every evening, and we sat by it with glasses of Jameson. Barrie reminisced about Tommy Flynn, who'd lived in a cottage by the lough and was a demon fiddler. Tommy once made a rod of greenheart wood from Guyana for the Queen Mother, and delivered it to Buckingham Palace himself. Then he told me a story about an old codger he met in Kilmactranny, who was idly moving rocks from one spot to another. When asked why, the codger replied, "To keep the archaeologists busy."

That was the only time I fished with Barrie, although we swapped letters—no email for Cooke—and angling info, and I met him frequently in Dublin at galleries and museums.

Shortly after our outing, he started traveling to New Zealand and Borneo where, he assured me, the best trout and salmon fishing in the world could be had. The lush jungle greens of the rainforests began to infuse his painting, and his late canvases glow with a subtropical warmth. Sadly, Barrie died in 2015 at the age of eighty-four, a year after his great friend Heaney, who wrote so admiringly of his work. I'll always be grateful to the kindness he showed to this wandering Californian.

13
The Magic Man

In the world of thoroughbred racing, Bob Baffert holds all the aces these days. No other trainer comes close to matching his recent success. Last year alone, his horses earned almost twelve million dollars in purse money. In 1997, Silver Charm, his star colt, won both the Kentucky Derby and the Preakness. Another colt, Real Quiet, did the same thing the following year. Baffert's rivals grumble about a secret weapon, but he says he just trusts his instincts and has extraordinary luck. That's another way of saying he's superstitious. He has certain neckties—power ties—that he'll wear only to big races. He refers to his favorite, a yellow Hermes, as "kick-ass." If a tie fails to deliver, it dies. Baffert stomped on one loser, and he invited his grooms to stomp on it. The tie was left behind in the dust, looking, he says, "as evil as a snake."

Baffert, at forty-six, is a slight man with prematurely white hair and a confident attitude. Being a creature of habit, he follows the same routine every day, driving from *his* home, in Huntington Beach, California, to Santa Anita, where he has forty horses stabled. His car is a new B.M.W. 740, with a sport package and a special Kentucky Derby license plate. He paid cash for the car, and doesn't care if you know that. His work clothes seldom vary—jeans, a plain shirt, boots, and, if the weather's cold, a navy-blue jacket—and he always has on funky little sunglasses, which hide his eyes and discourage interpretation. The tools of his trade are simple—a stopwatch, a two-way radio, and a cell phone that never stops ringing. "It's the nineties, buddy," he'll tell you, with a grin.

Most trainers are early birds, and get to the track around dawn, but Baffert comes a little later. His staff, of some fifty handpicked and well-paid people, takes care of the stock in his absence. The barn he's been assigned is close to a parking lot and easy for visitors to find. When I stopped by one morning in December, the operation was in full swing. I sat on a fence to wait for Baffert and watched some finches swoop around a pepper tree. The barn is an old wooden building with flaking green paint, and the silks of Silver Charm and Real Quiet are tacked up on it, in triumphant display. Hired hands were busy walking hots—horses just back from a gallop. I could smell manure and hear the horses breathing. It was impossible not to feel good.

Although the Triple Crown races were months away, Baffert was already gearing up for them. He hopes to win his third straight Derby, an unprecedented feat for a trainer, but the rate at which he has risen to the top of his field has also been unprecedented. When he started training thoroughbreds, in 1989, his stable consisted of a single horse—Hidden

Royalty, a thirty-two-thousand-dollar claimer—but now he handles colts as valuable as a Malibu beach house. He's so popular that owners beg *him* to take on their stock, and this can be a problem. Some owners don't listen very well. They have expectations and make demands. They don't heed the trainer's advice. If that happens, Baffert drops them. He hates stress, he told me once, because it gets in the way of having fun.

When Baffert arrived, we walked down to the track to watch the morning workouts. It was a beautiful day, bright and clear, and the San Gabriel Mountains stood out against a smogless sky. "Look at that!" Baffert said appreciatively. I followed *him* to a special spot by the grandstand, where he likes to hang out, far away from the other trainers. This may or may not be deliberate, but it adds to his mystique. His cell phone rang immediately, and he wandered off for a private chat. It could be anybody calling—someone from Dubai, where Silver Charm won the four-million-dollar World Cup last year, or maybe one of his four kids with a question—but his competitors would never know. Like the shades, that's part of his game plan. Baffert drives everybody nuts and gets a kick out of doing it.

On the track, his horses were flying by, offering a majestic pageant of muscle, speed, and color. Here came Silver Charm himself, a stunning gray, with his neck curled and his ears pricked, tugging away as if he wanted to run a hundred miles. Real Quiet rolled through next, more awkward-looking but just as game—a long-striding colt who, even as a four-year-old, may still be developing. Then Excellent Meeting and

Silverbulletday galloped past, a pair of brilliant fillies, whose coats shone in the sun. Baffert clocked them and oohed and ahed at the fractions. He was using his radio to instruct his exercise riders and monitor the action at his barn. To a Mexican jockey, he shouted encouragement in Spanish. He was at the hub of things, without ever moving an inch.

There's nothing like the right dream coming true. I could see how proud Baffert was. "Most powerful stable in North America," he said of his operation, not in a bragging way but as if he had his fingers crossed. He's still in awe of his good fortune. "Hope I don't blow it."

Bob Baffert grew up on a cattle ranch in Nogales, Arizona, with six brothers and sisters, but he was the only child who liked to ride. His favorite among the ranch's quarter horses was Baffert's Heller, a tough little customer. When Bob was ten, he would dash from the school bus to the corral and Lavish attention on him, but in the saddle the boy was scared, and the horse knew it. Heller always tried to buck him off. The ranch cowboys had no such trouble. Heller went easy on them, because they were grown men—and big—while Bob was small. "That's how smart horses are," he said. "They're usually sweet, but they can smell fear a mile away." With Heller, he mastered his fear at last, and from then on he rode the horse hard and well.

Baffert began training quarter horses in his teens, working for his father. He majored in animal sciences at the University of Arizona, and after he graduated, in 1977, he continued training horses as a hobby. He later decided to go pro, and ran his stock at dusty tracks around the Southwest. Those tracks were rough, and the crowd could be rowdy. Baffert did extremely well, but quarter horses aren't as challenging or complicated as thoroughbreds, and the races are strictly one-dimensional sprints. The longest covers only eight hundred and seventy yards. There wasn't much strategy involved, so Baffert kept getting bored. He'd take a job in the real world—as a substitute teacher, say, or selling livestock pharmaceutical supplies for a Tucson feed store—but the track always drew him back.

As we stood watching the horses, people drifted by and stopped to talk. Most of them wanted something from Baffert—a tip, a loan, a transfer of the magic. An elderly handicapper limped over, clutching a crumpled *Racing Form* that he'd decorated with runic symbols and spidery handwriting, the leavings of some arcane and almost certainly useless system. Baffert had a filly called Capote's Caper entered in the first race at Hollywood Park that afternoon, and asked how she looked. "Six lengths better than anybody else!" the old guy cried.

"Yeah, well," Baffert said, with a sigh. "The easy races are the toughest to win."

An agent for Chris McCarron, the great jockey, strolled up next. McCarron was scheduled to ride Prime Timber, one of Baffert's main Derby hopefuls, in the two-hundred-thousand-dollar-added Hollywood Futurity, on Saturday.

"McCarron's going to screw up tomorrow," Baffert said, teasing the agent. "He'll start thinking."

"He won't think," the agent promised.

To Baffert, a thinking jockey is as bad as a difficult owner or a drunken groom. As an example, he brought up the case of Kent Desormeaux, who booted home Real Quiet in the '98 Derby, at long-shot odds of eight to one. Desormeaux walked into the paddock at Churchill Downs on race day to talk with the boss about how he planned to ride. In the midst of julep-induced pandemonium, while Baffert's nerves were crackling, Desormeaux spouted theories and plotted tactics, waxing profound about the intricate journey he imagined for himself and his mount. Desormeaux was blatantly *thinking*, and Baffert couldn't believe it. "Cut it out, Kent!" he warned the jockey. "Believe me, son, you're on a loaded gun." That was the end of it, and Real Quiet wound up in the winner's circle.

It was Mike Pegram, Real Quiet's owner, who persuaded Baffert to jump from quarter horses into the big leagues. Baffert had moved his stable from Arizona to Southern California in 1983, and he had become a fixture at Los Alamitos, where he pulled down half a million in purses in 1990, but he was ready for a new challenge. Among the thoroughbreds he eventually bought and trained for Pegram was a Kentucky-bred that cost only seventeen thousand dollars at auction. The colt looked weirdly skinny from a head-on angle, as if he belonged in a tropical aquarium, so Baffert called him "the fish." As for Pegram, he thought the horse might have a terminal disease. This was Real Quiet, who went on to lose his first seven races.

There's no better testament to Baffert's patience and skill than the job he did with Real Quiet. Any trainer will stick with a classy prospect for a while, but most trainers tend to give up on cheap horses after a failure or two. Baffert saw a quality he liked, though, and he never doubted his intuition. He regards himself as a keen judge of character, even in horses, but he can't explain why. "I go by the feeling," he said. "I like a certain look, a certain conformation. I swear, I have ESP at times. Hey, I'm a real good gambler with other people's money." In Real Quiet he recognized a talented colt that needed room to grow, so he didn't push. The colt's progress was barely visible to outsiders, and when Baffert shipped him to a lowly New Mexico track for a race it was viewed as a sign of surrender. (The race was in fact a five-hundred- thousand-dollar stakes. Baffert enjoys competing in easier events in places other than California and refers to it as "taking the back road," but it didn't work this time. Even against lesser stock, Real Quiet lost once more.) Ultimately, the colt put on weight, became strong, quick, and durable, and repaid his trainer's faith many times over.

Because Baffert has performed such miracles, the experts figure he'll do even better now that he has horses with pedigrees. He tries to ignore the pressure, but it's there. Success on a grand scale can ruin a trainer. It forces him to be a businessman, and nobody on the backstretch is much interested in business. When Baffert began making money, his account books were in chaos until he hired a financial manager. He's suffering the first pangs of fame, too—the autograph-seekers, the glad-handers. "I can't go anywhere anymore," he complains. Celebrity goes against the grain of racetrack life, with its deep craving for simplicity and its low tolerance for affectation of any kind. Away from work, Baffert is most content when he's hanging out with his kids. Their names are Taylor, Canyon, Forest, and Savannah, and they never ask him for any inside information.

Still, Baffert can't avoid the fact that he has a sensational crop of three-year-olds in his barn. The one most respected at present is Exploit, whose sire, Storm Cat, is among the country's most expensive and desirable stallions. Bob and Beverly Lewis, who also own Silver Charm, paid five hundred and twenty-five thousand dollars for Exploit as a weanling. The notion was to pinhook him—sell him as a yearling— but no bidder met the reserve price of a million and a half dollars. (The bidding did reach a million four hundred and fifty thousand.) Baffert remained unconcerned. The colt had the build of a runner, he said, and that has proved to be an understatement. Exploit won his first four races handily, including a big victory in the Kentucky Jockey Club Stakes, at Churchill Downs, going around two turns.

When Exploit hit the track, Baffert took out his stopwatch and did some clocking. As the colt rushed by the grandstand, I had a chance to admire him up close. I thought Exploit looked splendid, working well within himself, effortlessly. He had a determined, energetic stride, his head down and his legs pumping.

"Does he look like a Derby horse to you?" Baffert asked. He didn't sound doubtful, just curious about the future. "He's on the small side, but he's got a lot of gas in his tank."

Toward the end of the workouts, we joined the crowd at the official Clockers' Corner, where the less secretive types gather to gossip. Baffert bought us some coffee and chatted with the woman behind the counter, who had been on vacation in the Sierra Nevada and boasted that she'd caught more trout than her husband had. A bloodstock agent cornered Baffert right after that to discuss the possibility of importing some horses from Argentina. Then a railbird butted in, claiming that he'd put down a big morning-line bet on Prime Timber at a Vegas casino.

"What were the odds?" Baffert wanted to know.

"Eighteen to one. I'm going to be a rich man on Derby Day," the railbird said smugly.

Baffert made no reply.

An exercise rider came over to pay court, his whip jammed in his back pocket. He had his little boy with him. The boy was about seven and wore a leather jacket so scraped up and abused that a truck might have mashed it.

"What do you want for Christmas?" Baffert asked. "Other than a new jacket, I mean."

The kid rolled with the punch. "When's Silver Charm gonna run again?" he asked.

"He looked good today, didn't he, buddy?"

"He looked beautiful."

"Well, I better find a race for him, then."

Baffert seldom points his horses toward a particular event. Instead, he lets them round into shape, and when they're prime and ready he shops for a race they have a chance of winning. This sounds elementary, but the condition book, as it is called, is probably the knottiest document at any track. It has nothing to do with the relative muddiness or dryness of the course. Instead, it sets out the conditions a horse must meet to enter a race, in language as dense as a brick. Some trainers never quite master it, but Baffert studies it diligently. The trick is not to aim too high and run a horse where it doesn't belong. "Can't make chicken salad out of chickenshit," Baffert likes to say.

We returned to his barn around ten. Hot-walkers were still at work, and a few colts and fillies were being bathed; steam came off them in the cool morning air. Before going on to his office, Baffert stuck his head into Silver Charm's stall and fed him some carrots. The office is unusually neat by racetrack standards, and has a fax and some computers. There were framed photographs of Baffert and Silver Charm after the Derby and the Preakness. He wore the same tie in both pictures. "I should have changed it for the Belmont," he said wistfully. "It would have been nice to earn the Triple Crown."

A horseshoer was at work just outside the door, hammering away in his leather chaps, and he let it drop that he'd shoed the last four Derby winners in a row.

"What's the record?" I asked him, joking.

He lifted his head to concentrate. "Somebody from Calumet Farm, I guess," he said. "Back when they used to win it every year."

Around eleven, Baffert fired up his BMW, and we left for Hollywood Park. Capote's Caper ran well in her race and led to the head of the stretch, only to be passed in the lane and finish second—an easy race that was tough to win, just as Baffert had predicted.

He didn't fare much better in the Futurity on Saturday. Prime Timber, undefeated in his only two starts, put on a good show, accelerating when McCarron asked him to, and taking command, bur Tactical Cat, a lightly regarded horse from D. Wayne Lukas's stable, nipped him at the wire. There was worse news for Baffert, though. Another colt he'd entered, Premier Property—a speedster who hadn't lost in three starts—tired at the distance, kept running anyway, and took a bad misstep, fracturing three metacarpal bones in his lower left foreleg. He had to be destroyed—a two-year-old in perfect condition snatched up in an instant, all for trying so hard.

"You never get used to that," Baffert told me later. "It's the most awful thing about racing, when you see a horse go down."

Baffert and Lukas are not exactly close pals. There's a keen edge of competition between them, so Baffert looked forward to another day. He got his chance for revenge in early February, when Exploit made his '99 debut, in the San Vicente Stakes, at Santa Anita, against Lukas's Yes It's True and a colt named Aristotle, from Randy Bradshaw's barn. The San Vicente is a prep race that everyone watches carefully, because six of its winners, including Silver Charm, have gone on to take the Derby. For Exploit it would be a return to the track after a long, ten-week layoff, but he still looked invincible in the paddock. Almost pure black, with white stockings banding three of his legs, he pranced and pricked his ears and could barely contain himself

A three-horse field puts extra pressure on a jockey, because tactics are of vital importance. Chris McCarron was concerned about Exploit's going too fast too soon, so for the early part of the race he let the colt settle at a moderate pace, in company with Yes It's True. But Lukas's entry couldn't get the seven-furlong distance and eventually faded, while Exploit went into overdrive. Just when it appeared that he might fly to the wire untested, Aristotle swooped into the picture. Down the stretch, the two horses were hooked, but Exploit showed his class by digging deep and finding the little bit extra he needed to win. It was a gritty performance, from a horse that was clearly something special. But how much had the effort cost him? We'd find out when he ran next, in the San Felipe Stakes, on March 13th.

Baffert savored the victory, but he knew how many obstacles he still had to surmount before buying any plane tickets to Louisville. The Derby was all about waiting, he said—waiting and luck. A trainer had to pray that one of his colts peaked at the right time. It could be Exploit or Prime Timber, Finder's Gold or General Challenge. The more prospects you had, the better your chances were. All Baffert could do was hope.

"The Kentucky Derby's the only race in the world," he told me. "I used to say I'd quit if I ever won it, but now I want to go every year. I don't drink or do drugs. That race is my addiction. It *motivates* me." He added that he always felt on edge during the post parade, and got more and more nervous until the moment when his horse was actually in the starting gate.

"What happens then?"

"Then I can relax," he said. "My job's done. Once the gate opens, there's nothing left to do but scream like hell."

Afterword

To bring matters up-to-date, I should say that Snow Chief failed in his Kentucky Derby bid, but Mel Stute is still a top trainer on the Southern California circuit. Although the Quarter Pole remains a day-to-day proposition, the jumpers can be counted on to scale the hedges and hurdles at Ascot in season, and the Queen Mother, now in her nineties, continues to cheer them on.

Mike Tyson's fate has unfolded much as I imagined it might. He is currently doing time for "road rage" and secured a permanent spot in the record books by biting off a chunk of Evander Holyfield's ear. Pat Lawlor did earn a title shot at last and took on J. D. Jackson of Seattle for the WBO Junior Middleweight belt, but he lost a decision, only to gain another boxing story for his repertoire.

I had no luck in tracing the Moscow Red Devils, yet I have a strong feeling that somehow—somewhere—Andrei Tzelikovsky is still going to the moon.